Cram101 Textbook Outlines to accompany:

Sport Management

Lussier and Kimball, 1st Edition

An Academic Internet Publishers (AIPI) publication (c) 2007.

You have a discounted membership at www.Cram101.com with this book.

Get all of the practice tests for the chapters of this textbook, and access in-depth reference material for writing essays and papers. Here is an example from a Cram101 Biology text:

When you need problem solving help with math, stats, and other disciplines, www.Cram101.com will walk through the formulas and solutions step by step.

With Cram101.com online, you also have access to extensive reference material.

You will nail those essays and papers. Here is an example from a Cram101 Biology text:

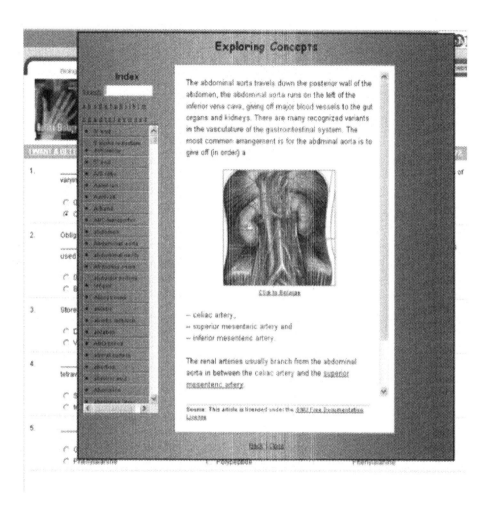

Visit **www.Cram101.com**, click Sign Up at the top of the screen, and enter DK73DW in the promo code box on the registration screen. Access to www.Cram101.com is normally $9.95, but because you have purchased this book, your access fee is only $4.95. Sign up and stop highlighting textbooks forever.

Learning System

Cram101 Textbook Outlines is a learning system. The notes in this book are the highlights of your textbook, you will never have to highlight a book again.

How to use this book. Take this book to class, it is your notebook for the lecture. The notes and highlights on the left hand side of the pages follow the outline and order of the textbook. All you have to do is follow along while your intructor presents the lecture. Circle the items emphasized in class and add other important information on the right side. With Cram101 Textbook Outlines you'll spend less time writing and more time listening. Learning becomes more efficient.

Cram101.com Online

Increase your studying efficiency by using Cram101.com's practice tests and online reference material. It is the perfect complement to Cram101 Textbook Outlines. Use self-teaching matching tests or simulate in-class testing with comprehensive multiple choice tests, or simply use Cram's true and false tests for quick review. Cram101.com even allows you to enter your in-class notes for an integrated studying format combining the textbook notes with your class notes.

Visit **www.Cram101.com**, click Sign Up at the top of the screen, and enter **DK73DW430** in the promo code box on the registration screen. Access to www.Cram101.com is normally $9.95, but because you have purchased this book, your access fee is only $4.95. Sign up and stop highlighting textbooks forever.

Sport Management
Lussier and Kimball, 1st

CONTENTS

Management	Management characterizes the process of leading and directing all or part of an organization, often a business, through the deployment and manipulation of resources. Early twentieth-century management writer Mary Parker Follett defined management as "the art of getting things done through people."
Project manager	Project manager refers to a manager responsible for a temporary work project that involves the participation of other people from various functions and levels of the organization.
Leadership	Management merely consists of leadership applied to business situations; or in other words: management forms a sub-set of the broader process of leadership.
Industry	A group of firms that produce identical or similar products is an industry. It is also used specifically to refer to an area of economic production focused on manufacturing which involves large amounts of capital investment before any profit can be realized, also called "heavy industry".
Economy	The income, expenditures, and resources that affect the cost of running a business and household are called an economy.
General manager	A manager who is responsible for several departments that perform different functions is called general manager.
Operation	A standardized method or technique that is performed repetitively, often on different materials resulting in different finished goods is called an operation.
Marketing	Promoting and selling products or services to customers, or prospective customers, is referred to as marketing.
Sponsorship	When the advertiser assumes responsibility for the production and usually the content of a television program as well as the advertising that appears within it, we have sponsorship.
Gain	In finance, gain is a profit or an increase in value of an investment such as a stock or bond. Gain is calculated by fair market value or the proceeds from the sale of the investment minus the sum of the purchase price and all costs associated with it.
Agent	A person who makes economic decisions for another economic actor. A hired manager operates as an agent for a firm's owner.
Human resources	Human resources refers to the individuals within the firm, and to the portion of the firm's organization that deals with hiring, firing, training, and other personnel issues.
Purchasing	Purchasing refers to the function in a firm that searches for quality material resources, finds the best suppliers, and negotiates the best price for goods and services.
Authority	Authority in agency law, refers to an agent's ability to affect his principal's legal relations with third parties. Also used to refer to an actor's legal power or ability to do something. In addition, sometimes used to refer to a statute, case, or other legal source that justifies a particular result.
Manufacturing	Production of goods primarily by the application of labor and capital to raw materials and other intermediate inputs, in contrast to agriculture, mining, forestry, fishing, and services a manufacturing.
Retailing	All activities involved in selling, renting, and providing goods and services to ultimate consumers for personal, family, or household use is referred to as retailing.
Fund	Independent accounting entity with a self-balancing set of accounts segregated for the purposes of carrying on specific activities is referred to as a fund.
Budget	Budget refers to an account, usually for a year, of the planned expenditures and the expected receipts of an entity. For a government, the receipts are tax revenues.
Physical resources	Natural resources used in the transformation process to create resources of more value are called physical resources.

Supply	Supply is the aggregate amount of any material good that can be called into being at a certain price point; it comprises one half of the equation of supply and demand. In classical economic theory, a curve representing supply is one of the factors that produce price.
Gallup Poll	The Gallup Poll has existed since the 1930s. Historically, it has measured and tracked the public's attitudes concerning virtually every political, social, and economic issue of the day, including highly sensitive or controversial subjects. Typically it uses a simple random sampling method in order to keep the level of bias to a minimum.
Conceptual skill	The ability to analyze and solve complex problems is called conceptual skill. Conceptual skill involves the formulation of ideas.
Skills management	Skills Management is the practice of understanding, developing and deploying people and their skills. Well-implemented skills management should identify the skills that job roles require, the skills of individual employees, and any gap between the two.
Speculation	The purchase or sale of an asset in hopes that its price will rise or fall respectively, in order to make a profit is called speculation.
Accounting	A system that collects and processes financial information about an organization and reports that information to decision makers is referred to as accounting.
Stakeholder	A stakeholder is an individual or group with a vested interest in or expectation for organizational performance. Usually stakeholders can either have an effect on or are affected by an organization.
Market	A market is, as defined in economics, a social arrangement that allows buyers and sellers to discover information and carry out a voluntary exchange of goods or services.
Marketing strategy	Marketing strategy refers to the means by which a marketing goal is to be achieved, usually characterized by a specified target market and a marketing program to reach it.
Controlling	A management function that involves determining whether or not an organization is progressing toward its goals and objectives, and taking corrective action if it is not is called controlling.
Management functions	Management functions were set forth by Henri Fayol; they include planning, organizing, leading, and controling.
Allocate	Allocate refers to the assignment of income for various tax purposes. A multistate corporation's nonbusiness income usually is distributed to the state where the nonbusiness assets are located; it is not apportioned with the rest of the entity's income.
Staffing	Staffing refers to a management function that includes hiring, motivating, and retaining the best people available to accomplish the company's objectives.
Interpersonal roles	In management there are three important interpersonal roles: the figurehead, the leader, and the liaison.
Liaison	An individual who serves as a bridge between groups, tying groups together and facilitating the communication flow needed to integrate group activities is a liaison.
Resource allocator	A resource allocator is a plan for using available resources, for example human resources, especially in the near term, to achieve goals for the future. It is the process of allocating resources among the various projects or business units.
Entrepreneur	The owner/operator. The person who organizes, manages, and assumes the risks of a firm, taking a new idea or a new product and turning it into a successful business is an entrepreneur.
Service	Service refers to a "non tangible product" that is not embodied in a physical good and that typically effects some change in another product, person, or institution. Contrasts with good.
Technology	The body of knowledge and techniques that can be used to combine economic resources to produce goods and services is called technology.

Nonprofit organization	An organization whose goals do not include making a personal profit for its owners is a nonprofit organization.
Hierarchy	A system of grouping people in an organization according to rank from the top down in which all subordinate managers must report to one person is called a hierarchy.
Chief executive officer	A chief executive officer is the highest-ranking corporate officer or executive officer of a corporation, or agency. In closely held corporations, it is general business culture that the office chief executive officer is also the chairman of the board.
Holding	The holding is a court's determination of a matter of law based on the issue presented in the particular case. In other words: under this law, with these facts, this result.
Functional manager	A manager who is responsible for a department that performs a single functional task and has employees with similar training and skills is referred to as a functional manager.
Production	The creation of finished goods and services using the factors of production: land, labor, capital, entrepreneurship, and knowledge.
Advertising	Advertising refers to paid, nonpersonal communication through various media by organizations and individuals who are in some way identified in the advertising message.
Accounts receivable	Accounts receivable is one of a series of accounting transactions dealing with the billing of customers which owe money to a person, company or organization for goods and services that have been provided to the customer. This is typically done in a one person organization by writing an invoice and mailing or delivering it to each customer.
Financial manager	Managers who make recommendations to top executives regarding strategies for improving the financial strength of a firm are referred to as a financial manager.
Expense	In accounting, an expense represents an event in which an asset is used up or a liability is incurred. In terms of the accounting equation, expenses reduce owners' equity.
Financing activities	Cash flow activities that include obtaining cash from issuing debt and repaying the amounts borrowed and obtaining cash from stockholders and paying dividends is referred to as financing activities.
Balance	In banking and accountancy, the outstanding balance is the amount of money owned, (or due), that remains in a deposit account (or a loan account) at a given date, after all past remittances, payments and withdrawal have been accounted for. It can be positive (then, in the balance sheet of a firm, it is an asset) or negative (a liability).
Administration	Administration refers to the management and direction of the affairs of governments and institutions; a collective term for all policymaking officials of a government; the execution and implementation of public policy.
Small business	Small business refers to a business that is independently owned and operated, is not dominant in its field of operation, and meets certain standards of size in terms of employees or annual receipts.
Organization structure	The system of task, reporting, and authority relationships within which the organization does its work is referred to as the organization structure.
Formal organization	Formal organization refers to the structure that details lines of responsibility, authority, and position; that is, the structure shown on organization charts.
Policy	Similar to a script in that a policy can be a less than completely rational decision-making method. Involves the use of a pre-existing set of decision steps for any problem that presents itself.
Control system	A control system is a device or set of devices that manage the behavior of other devices. Some devices or systems are not controllable. A control system is an interconnection of components connected or related in such a manner as to command, direct, or regulate itself or another system.
Profit	Profit refers to the return to the resource entrepreneurial ability; total revenue minus total cost.

Go to **Cram101.com** for the Practice Tests for this Chapter.

Margin	A deposit by a buyer in stocks with a seller or a stockbroker, as security to cover fluctuations in the market in reference to stocks that the buyer has purchased but for which he has not paid is a margin. Commodities are also traded on margin.
Nike	Because Nike creates goods for a wide range of sports, they have competition from every sports and sports fashion brand there is. Nike has no direct competitors because there is no single brand which can compete directly with their range of sports and non-sports oriented gear, except for Reebok.
Corporation	A legal entity chartered by a state or the Federal government that is distinct and separate from the individuals who own it is a corporation. This separation gives the corporation unique powers which other legal entities lack.
Sweatshop	A sweatshop is a factory or workshop that has attributes in common with the workplaces of the pejoratively-named sweating system of the 1840s. Sweatshops arose at a time when workers did not have the protections afforded by trade unions or labor laws, and sweatshops are synonymous with working conditions that violate human rights sensibilities and sometimes public policies. .
Management team	A management team is directly responsible for managing the day-to-day operations (and profitability) of a company.
Developing country	Developing country refers to a country whose per capita income is low by world standards. Same as LDC. As usually used, it does not necessarily connote that the country's income is rising.
Labor	People's physical and mental talents and efforts that are used to help produce goods and services are called labor.
Wage	The payment for the service of a unit of labor, per unit time. In trade theory, it is the only payment to labor, usually unskilled labor. In empirical work, wage data may exclude other compenzation, which must be added to get the total cost of employment.
Adidas	Adidas is a German sports apparel manufacturer, part of the Adidas Group. The company was named after its founder, Adolf Dassler, who started producing shoes in the 1920s in Herzogenaurach near Nuremberg with the help of his brother Rudolf Dassler who later formed rival shoe company PUMA AG.

Go to **Cram101.com** for the Practice Tests for this Chapter.

Total quality management	The broad set of management and control processes designed to focus an entire organization and all of its employees on providing products or services that do the best possible job of satisfying the customer is called total quality management.
Quality management	Quality management is a method for ensuring that all the activities necessary to design, develop and implement a product or service are effective and efficient with respect to the system and its performance.
Management	Management characterizes the process of leading and directing all or part of an organization, often a business, through the deployment and manipulation of resources. Early twentieth-century management writer Mary Parker Follett defined management as "the art of getting things done through people."
Domestic	From or in one's own country. A domestic producer is one that produces inside the home country. A domestic price is the price inside the home country. Opposite of 'foreign' or 'world.'.
Stakeholder	A stakeholder is an individual or group with a vested interest in or expectation for organizational performance. Usually stakeholders can either have an effect on or are affected by an organization.
Social responsibility	Social responsibility is a doctrine that claims that an entity whether it is state, government, corporation, organization or individual has a responsibility to society.
Reengineering	The fundamental rethinking and redesign of business processes to achieve improvements in critical measures of performance, such as cost, quality, service, speed, and customer satisfaction is referred to as reengineering.
Downsizing	The process of eliminating managerial and non-managerial positions are called downsizing.
Shill	A shill is an associate of a person selling goods or services, who pretends no association to the seller and assumes the air of an enthusiastic customer.
Heir	In common law jurisdictions an heir is a person who is entitled to receive a share of the decedent's property via the rules of inheritance in the jurisdiction where the decedent died or owned property at the time of his death.
Inventory	Tangible property held for sale in the normal course of business or used in producing goods or services for sale is an inventory.
Competitor	Other organizations in the same industry or type of business that provide a good or service to the same set of customers is referred to as a competitor.
Internal environment	Variables that are under some degree of control by organizational members is the internal enviroment. Internal environment scans are conducted to identify an organization's internal capabilities, performance levels, strengths, and weaknesses.
Nonprofit organization	An organization whose goals do not include making a personal profit for its owners is a nonprofit organization.
Service	Service refers to a "non tangible product" that is not embodied in a physical good and that typically effects some change in another product, person, or institution. Contrasts with good.
Profit	Profit refers to the return to the resource entrepreneurial ability; total revenue minus total cost.
Leadership	Management merely consists of leadership applied to business situations; or in other words: management forms a sub-set of the broader process of leadership.
Business	A business opportunity involves the sale or lease of any product, service, equipment, etc.

Go to **Cram101.com** for the Practice Tests for this Chapter.

opportunity	that will enable the purchaser-licensee to begin a business
Effective manager	Leader of a team that consistently achieves high performance goals is an effective manager.
Market	A market is, as defined in economics, a social arrangement that allows buyers and sellers to discover information and carry out a voluntary exchange of goods or services.
Mission statement	Mission statement refers to an outline of the fundamental purposes of an organization.
Consultant	A professional that provides expert advice in a particular field or area in which customers occassionaly require this type of knowledge is a consultant.
Organizational Behavior	The study of human behavior in organizational settings, the interface between human behavior and the organization, and the organization itself is called organizational behavior.
Interest	In finance and economics, interest is the price paid by a borrower for the use of a lender's money. In other words, interest is the amount of paid to "rent" money for a period of time.
Human resources	Human resources refers to the individuals within the firm, and to the portion of the firm's organization that deals with hiring, firing, training, and other personnel issues.
Physical resources	Natural resources used in the transformation process to create resources of more value are called physical resources.
Inputs	The inputs used by a firm or an economy are the labor, raw materials, electricity and other resources it uses to produce its outputs.
Complement	A good that is used in conjunction with another good is a complement. For example, cameras and film would complement eachother.
Production	The creation of finished goods and services using the factors of production: land, labor, capital, entrepreneurship, and knowledge.
Personnel	A collective term for all of the employees of an organization. Personnel is also commonly used to refer to the personnel management function or the organizational unit responsible for administering personnel programs.
Marketing	Promoting and selling products or services to customers, or prospective customers, is referred to as marketing.
Management philosophy	Management philosophy refers to a philosophy that links key goal-related issues with key collaboration issues to come up with general ways by which the firm will manage its affairs.
Shareholder	A shareholder is an individual or company (including a corporation) that legally owns one or more shares of stock in a joined stock company.
Technology	The body of knowledge and techniques that can be used to combine economic resources to produce goods and services is called technology.
Economy	The income, expenditures, and resources that affect the cost of running a business and household are called an economy.
Customer value	Customer value refers to the unique combination of benefits received by targeted buyers that includes quality, price, convenience, on-time delivery, and both before-sale and after-sale service.
Industry	A group of firms that produce identical or similar products is an industry. It is also used specifically to refer to an area of economic production focused on manufacturing which involves large amounts of capital investment before any profit can be realized, also called "heavy industry".

Market share	That fraction of an industry's output accounted for by an individual firm or group of firms is called market share.
Brand	A name, symbol, or design that identifies the goods or services of one seller or group of sellers and distinguishes them from the goods and services of competitors is a brand.
Firm	An organization that employs resources to produce a good or service for profit and owns and operates one or more plants is referred to as a firm.
Business strategy	Business strategy, which refers to the aggregated operational strategies of single business firm or that of an SBU in a diversified corporation refers to the way in which a firm competes in its chosen arenas.
Gain	In finance, gain is a profit or an increase in value of an investment such as a stock or bond. Gain is calculated by fair market value or the proceeds from the sale of the investment minus the sum of the purchase price and all costs associated with it.
Nike	Because Nike creates goods for a wide range of sports, they have competition from every sports and sports fashion brand there is. Nike has no direct competitors because there is no single brand which can compete directly with their range of sports and non-sports oriented gear, except for Reebok.
Labor	People's physical and mental talents and efforts that are used to help produce goods and services are called labor.
Union	A worker association that bargains with employers over wages and working conditions is called a union.
Goodwill	Goodwill is an important accounting concept that describes the value of a business entity not directly attributable to its tangible assets and liabilities.
Revenue	Revenue is a U.S. business term for the amount of money that a company receives from its activities, mostly from sales of products and/or services to customers.
Strike	The withholding of labor services by an organized group of workers is referred to as a strike.
Wage	The payment for the service of a unit of labor, per unit time. In trade theory, it is the only payment to labor, usually unskilled labor. In empirical work, wage data may exclude other compenzation, which must be added to get the total cost of employment.
Corporation	A legal entity chartered by a state or the Federal government that is distinct and separate from the individuals who own it is a corporation. This separation gives the corporation unique powers which other legal entities lack.
A share	In finance the term A share has two distinct meanings, both relating to securities. The first is a designation for a 'class' of common or preferred stock. A share of common or preferred stock typically has enhanced voting rights or other benefits compared to the other forms of shares that may have been created. The equity structure, or how many types of shares are offered, is determined by the corporate charter.
Stock	In financial terminology, stock is the capital raized by a corporation, through the issuance and sale of shares.
Board of directors	The group of individuals elected by the stockholders of a corporation to oversee its operations is a board of directors.
Chief executive officer	A chief executive officer is the highest-ranking corporate officer or executive officer of a corporation, or agency. In closely held corporations, it is general business culture that the office chief executive officer is also the chairman of the board.

Go to **Cram101.com** for the Practice Tests for this Chapter.

Chief financial officer	Chief financial officer refers to executive responsible for overseeing the financial operations of an organization.
Disney	Disney is one of the largest media and entertainment corporations in the world. Founded on October 16, 1923 by brothers Walt and Roy Disney as a small animation studio, today it is one of the largest Hollywood studios and also owns nine theme parks and several television networks, including the American Broadcasting Company (ABC).
Context	The effect of the background under which a message often takes on more and richer meaning is a context. Context is especially important in cross-cultural interactions because some cultures are said to be high context or low context.
Technological change	The introduction of new methods of production or new products intended to increase the productivity of existing inputs or to raise marginal products is a technological change.
Operation	A standardized method or technique that is performed repetitively, often on different materials resulting in different finished goods is called an operation.
Foreign exchange	In finance, foreign exchange means currencies, such as U.S. Dollars and Euros. These are traded on foreign exchange markets.
Economic growth	Economic growth refers to the increase over time in the capacity of an economy to produce goods and services and to improve the well-being of its citizens.
Interest rate	The rate of return on bonds, loans, or deposits. When one speaks of 'the' interest rate, it is usually in a model where there is only one.
Exchange rate	Exchange rate refers to the price at which one country's currency trades for another, typically on the exchange market.
Inflation	An increase in the overall price level of an economy, usually as measured by the CPI or by the implicit price deflator is called inflation.
Exchange	The trade of things of value between buyer and seller so that each is better off after the trade is called the exchange.
Gross domestic product	Gross domestic product refers to the total value of new goods and services produced in a given year within the borders of a country, regardless of by whom.
Recession	A significant decline in economic activity. In the U.S., recession is approximately defined as two successive quarters of falling GDP, as judged by NBER.
Economics	The social science dealing with the use of scarce resources to obtain the maximum satisfaction of society's virtually unlimited economic wants is an economics.
Creative strategy	A determination of what an advertising message will say or communicate to a target audience is called creative strategy.
Regulation	Regulation refers to restrictions state and federal laws place on business with regard to the conduct of its activities.
Closing	The finalization of a real estate sales transaction that passes title to the property from the seller to the buyer is referred to as a closing. Closing is a sales term which refers to the process of making a sale. It refers to reaching the final step, which may be an exchange of money or acquiring a signature.
General manager	A manager who is responsible for several departments that perform different functions is called general manager.
Antitrust	Government intervention to alter market structure or prevent abuse of market power is called antitrust.

Team cohesiveness	The extent to which team members are attracted to the team and motivated to remain in it is called team cohesiveness.
Complexity	The technical sophistication of the product and hence the amount of understanding required to use it is referred to as complexity. It is the opposite of simplicity.
Globalization of markets	Moving away from an economic system in which national markets are distinct entities, isolated by trade barriers and barriers of distance, time, and culture, and toward a system in which national markets are merging into one global market is globalization of markets.
Globalization	The increasing world-wide integration of markets for goods, services and capital that attracted special attention in the late 1990s is called globalization.
Management system	A management system is the framework of processes and procedures used to ensure that an organization can fulfill all tasks required to achieve its objectives.
North American Free Trade Agreement	A 1993 agreement establishing, over a 15-year period, a free trade zone composed of Canada, Mexico, and the United States is referred to as the North American Free Trade Agreement.
Free trade	Free trade refers to a situation in which there are no artificial barriers to trade, such as tariffs and quotas. Usually used, often only implicitly, with frictionless trade, so that it implies that there are no barriers to trade of any kind.
International Business	International business refers to any firm that engages in international trade or investment.
Adidas	Adidas is a German sports apparel manufacturer, part of the Adidas Group. The company was named after its founder, Adolf Dassler, who started producing shoes in the 1920s in Herzogenaurach near Nuremberg with the help of his brother Rudolf Dassler who later formed rival shoe company PUMA AG.
Multinational corporations	Firms that own production facilities in two or more countries and produce and sell their products globally are referred to as multinational corporations.
Multinational corporation	An organization that manufactures and markets products in many different countries and has multinational stock ownership and multinational management is referred to as multinational corporation.
Transnational	Transnational focuses on the heightened interconnectivity between people all around the world and the loosening of boundaries between countries.
Committee	A long-lasting, sometimes permanent team in the organization structure created to deal with tasks that recur regularly is the committee.
Outsourcing	Outsourcing refers to a production activity that was previously done inside a firm or plant that is now conducted outside that firm or plant.
Maquiladora	A maquiladora is a factory that imports materials and equipment on a duty-free and tariff-free basis for assembly or manufacturing and then re-exports the assembled product usually back to the originating country.
Exporting	Selling products to another country is called exporting.
Export	In economics, an export is any good or commodity, shipped or otherwise transported out of a country, province, town to another part of the world in a legitimate fashion, typically for use in trade or sale.
Licensing agreement	Detailed and comprehensive written agreement between the licensor and licensee that sets forth the express terms of their agreement is called a licensing agreement.
Licensing	Licensing is a form of strategic alliance which involves the sale of a right to use certain

Go to **Cram101.com** for the Practice Tests for this Chapter.

proprietary knowledge (so called intellectual property) in a defined way.

Trademark	A distinctive word, name, symbol, device, or combination thereof, which enables consumers to identify favored products or services and which may find protection under state or federal law is a trademark.
Copyright	The legal right to the proceeds from and control over the use of a created product, such a written work, audio, video, film, or software is a copyright. This right generally extends over the life of the author plus fifty years.
Patent	The legal right to the proceeds from and control over the use of an invented product or process, granted for a fixed period of time, usually 20 years. Patent is one form of intellectual property that is subject of the TRIPS agreement.
Asset	An item of property, such as land, capital, money, a share in ownership, or a claim on others for future payment, such as a bond or a bank deposit is an asset.
Contract manufacturing	Contract manufacturing refers to a foreign country's production of private-label goods to which a domestic company then attaches its brand name or trademark; also called outsourcing.
Manufacturing	Production of goods primarily by the application of labor and capital to raw materials and other intermediate inputs, in contrast to agriculture, mining, forestry, fishing, and services a manufacturing.
Contract	A contract is a "promise" or an "agreement" that is enforced or recognized by the law. In the civil law, a contract is considered to be part of the general law of obligations.
Joint venture	Joint venture refers to an undertaking by two parties for a specific purpose and duration, taking any of several legal forms.
Partnership	In the common law, a partnership is a type of business entity in which partners share with each other the profits or losses of the business undertaking in which they have all invested.
Enterprise	Enterprise refers to another name for a business organization. Other similar terms are business firm, sometimes simply business, sometimes simply firm, as well as company, and entity.
Sponsorship	When the advertiser assumes responsibility for the production and usually the content of a television program as well as the advertising that appears within it, we have sponsorship.
Direct investment	Direct investment refers to a domestic firm actually investing in and owning a foreign subsidiary or division.
Subsidiary	A company that is controlled by another company or corporation is a subsidiary.
Investment	Investment refers to spending for the production and accumulation of capital and additions to inventories. In a financial sense, buying an asset with the expectation of making a return.
Chief operating officer	A chief operating officer is a corporate officer responsible for managing the day-to-day activities of the corporation. The chief operating officer is one of the highest ranking members of an organization, monitoring the daily operations of the company and reporting to the chief executive officer directly.
Security	Security refers to a claim on the borrower future income that is sold by the borrower to the lender. A security is a type of transferable interest representing financial value.
Transcript	A copy of writing is referred to as a transcript. It is the official record of proceedings in a trial or hearing.
Trust	An arrangement in which shareholders of independent firms agree to give up their stock in exchange for trust certificates that entitle them to a share of the trust's common profits.

Go to **Cram101.com** for the Practice Tests for this Chapter.

Infraction	Infraction is an essentially minor violation of law where the penalty upon conviction only consists of monetary forfeiture. A violation of law which could include imprisonment is a crime. It is distinguished from a misdemeanor or a felony in that the penalty for an infraction cannot include any imprisonment.
Ethics committee	A group of executives assigned to oversee the organization's ethics by ruling on questionable issues and disciplining violators are called the ethics committee.
Layoff	A layoff is the termination of an employee or (more commonly) a group of employees for business reasons, such as the decision that certain positions are no longer necessary.
Outplacement	The process of placing employees in other positions or training once they have been separated from a job is outplacement. It helps people regain employment elsewhere.
Assessment	Collecting information and providing feedback to employees about their behavior, communication style, or skills is an assessment.
Preparation	Preparation refers to usually the first stage in the creative process. It includes education and formal training.
Frequency	Frequency refers to the speed of the up and down movements of a fluctuating economic variable; that is, the number of times per unit of time that the variable completes a cycle of up and down movement.
Assignment	A transfer of property or some right or interest is referred to as assignment.
Expense	In accounting, an expense represents an event in which an asset is used up or a liability is incurred. In terms of the accounting equation, expenses reduce owners' equity.
Sexual harassment	Unwelcome sexual advances, requests for sexual favors, and other conduct of a sexual nature is called sexual harassment.
Complaint	The pleading in a civil case in which the plaintiff states his claim and requests relief is called complaint. In the common law, it is a formal legal document that sets out the basic facts and legal reasons that the filing party (the plaintiffs) believes are sufficient to support a claim against another person, persons, entity or entities (the defendants) that entitles the plaintiff(s) to a remedy (either money damages or injunctive relief).
Policy	Similar to a script in that a policy can be a less than completely rational decision-making method. Involves the use of a pre-existing set of decision steps for any problem that presents itself.
Trend	Trend refers to the long-term movement of an economic variable, such as its average rate of increase or decrease over enough years to encompass several business cycles.
Authority	Authority in agency law, refers to an agent's ability to affect his principal's legal relations with third parties. Also used to refer to an actor's legal power or ability to do something. In addition, sometimes used to refer to a statute, case, or other legal source that justifies a particular result.
Administrator	Administrator refers to the personal representative appointed by a probate court to settle the estate of a deceased person who died.
Conflict of interest	A conflict that occurs when a corporate officer or director enters into a transaction with the corporation in which he or she has a personal interest is a conflict of interest.
Compromise	Compromise occurs when the interaction is moderately important to meeting goals and the goals are neither completely compatible nor completely incompatible.
Privilege	Generally, a legal right to engage in conduct that would otherwise result in legal liability is a privilege. Privileges are commonly classified as absolute or conditional. Occasionally,

22

Go to **Cram101.com** for the Practice Tests for this Chapter.

	privilege is also used to denote a legal right to refrain from particular behavior.
Cooperative	A business owned and controlled by the people who use it, producers, consumers, or workers with similar needs who pool their resources for mutual gain is called cooperative.
Retail sale	The sale of goods and services to consumers for their own use is a retail sale.
Bid	A bid price is a price offered by a buyer when he/she buys a good. In the context of stock trading on a stock exchange, the bid price is the highest price a buyer of a stock is willing to pay for a share of that given stock.
Adam Smith	Adam Smith (baptized June 5, 1723 O.S. (June 16 N.S.) – July 17, 1790) was a Scottish political economist and moral philosopher. His Inquiry into the Nature and Causes of the Wealth of Nations was one of the earliest attempts to study the historical development of industry and commerce in Europe. That work helped to create the modern academic discipline of economics
Capitalism	Capitalism refers to an economic system in which capital is mostly owned by private individuals and corporations. Contrasts with communism.
Public interest	The universal label that political actors wrap around the policies and programs that they advocate is referred to as public interest.
Long run	In economic models, the long run time frame assumes no fixed factors of production. Firms can enter or leave the marketplace, and the cost (and availability) of land, labor, raw materials, and capital goods can be assumed to vary.
Milton Friedman	Milton Friedman (born July 31, 1912) is an American economist, known for his work on macroeconomics, microeconomics, economic history, statistics, and for his advocacy of laissez-faire capitalism. In 1976 he won the Nobel Memorial Prize in Economics for his achievements in the fields of consumption analysis, monetary history and theory and for his demonstration of the complexity of stabilization policy.
Compliance	A type of influence process where a receiver accepts the position advocated by a source to obtain favorable outcomes or to avoid punishment is the compliance.
Corporate citizenship	A theory of responsibility that says a business has a responsibility to do good is corporate citizenship. Terms used in the business sector to refer to business giving, ie. business relationships and partnerships with not-for-profit organizations.
Audit	An examination of the financial reports to ensure that they represent what they claim and conform with generally accepted accounting principles is referred to as audit.
Annual report	An annual report is prepared by corporate management that presents financial information including financial statements, footnotes, and the management discussion and analysis.
Productivity	Productivity refers to the total output of goods and services in a given period of time divided by work hours.
Participative management	Participative management or participatory management is the practice of empowering employees to participate in organizational decision making.
International firm	International firm refers to those firms who have responded to stiff competition domestically by expanding their sales abroad. They may start a production facility overseas and send some of their managers, who report to a global division, to that country.
Margin	A deposit by a buyer in stocks with a seller or a stockbroker, as security to cover fluctuations in the market in reference to stocks that the buyer has purchased but for which he has not paid is a margin. Commodities are also traded on margin.
Purchasing	Purchasing refers to the function in a firm that searches for quality material resources,

	finds the best suppliers, and negotiates the best price for goods and services.
Multinational enterprise	Multinational enterprise refers to a firm, usually a corporation, that operates in two or more countries.
Bribery	When one person gives another person money, property, favors, or anything else of value for a favor in return, we have bribery. Often referred to as a payoff or 'kickback.'
Corruption	The unauthorized use of public office for private gain. The most common forms of corruption are bribery, extortion, and the misuse of inside information.
Organizational environment	Organizational environment refers to everything outside an organization. It includes all elements, people, other organizations, economic factors, objects, and events that lie outside the boundaries of the organization.
Niche	In industry, a niche is a situation or an activity perfectly suited to a person. A niche can imply a working position or an area suited to a person who occupies it. Basically, a job where a person is able to succeed and thrive.

Go to **Cram101.com** for the Practice Tests for this Chapter.

Management functions	Management functions were set forth by Henri Fayol; they include planning, organizing, leading, and controling.
Management	Management characterizes the process of leading and directing all or part of an organization, often a business, through the deployment and manipulation of resources. Early twentieth-century management writer Mary Parker Follett defined management as "the art of getting things done through people."
Nonprogrammed decision	Nonprogrammed decision refers to a decision that recurs infrequently and for which there is no previously established decision rule.
Decision support system	An interactive, computer-based system that uses decision models and specialized databases to support decision makers is called a decision support system.
Information technology	Information technology refers to technology that helps companies change business by allowing them to use new methods.
Technology	The body of knowledge and techniques that can be used to combine economic resources to produce goods and services is called technology.
Effective manager	Leader of a team that consistently achieves high performance goals is an effective manager.
WorldCom	WorldCom was the United States' second largest long distance phone company (AT&T was the largest). WorldCom grew largely by acquiring other telecommunications companies, most notably MCI Communications. It also owned the Tier 1 ISP UUNET, a major part of the Internet backbone.
Economy	The income, expenditures, and resources that affect the cost of running a business and household are called an economy.
Xerox	Xerox was founded in 1906 as "The Haloid Company" manufacturing photographic paper and equipment. The company came to prominence in 1959 with the introduction of the first plain paper photocopier using the process of xerography (electrophotography) developed by Chester Carlson, the Xerox 914.
Enron	Enron Corportaion's global reputation was undermined by persistent rumours of bribery and political pressure to secure contracts in Central America, South America, Africa, and the Philippines. Especially controversial was its $3 billion contract with the Maharashtra State Electricity Board in India, where it is alleged that Enron officials used political connections within the Clinton and Bush administrations to exert pressure on the board.
Corporation	A legal entity chartered by a state or the Federal government that is distinct and separate from the individuals who own it is a corporation. This separation gives the corporation unique powers which other legal entities lack.
Industry	A group of firms that produce identical or similar products is an industry. It is also used specifically to refer to an area of economic production focused on manufacturing which involves large amounts of capital investment before any profit can be realized, also called "heavy industry".
License	A license in the sphere of Intellectual Property Rights (IPR) is a document, contract or agreement giving permission or the 'right' to a legally-definable entity to do something (such as manufacture a product or to use a service), or to apply something (such as a trademark), with the objective of achieving commercial gain.
Nike	Because Nike creates goods for a wide range of sports, they have competition from every sports and sports fashion brand there is. Nike has no direct competitors because there is no single brand which can compete directly with their range of sports and non-sports oriented gear, except for Reebok.

Go to **Cram101.com** for the Practice Tests for this Chapter.

Labor	People's physical and mental talents and efforts that are used to help produce goods and services are called labor.
Brand	A name, symbol, or design that identifies the goods or services of one seller or group of sellers and distinguishes them from the goods and services of competitors is a brand.
Gap	In December of 1995, Gap became the first major North American retailer to accept independent monitoring of the working conditions in a contract factory producing its garments. Gap is the largest specialty retailer in the United States.
Adidas	Adidas is a German sports apparel manufacturer, part of the Adidas Group. The company was named after its founder, Adolf Dassler, who started producing shoes in the 1920s in Herzogenaurach near Nuremberg with the help of his brother Rudolf Dassler who later formed rival shoe company PUMA AG.
Customer value	Customer value refers to the unique combination of benefits received by targeted buyers that includes quality, price, convenience, on-time delivery, and both before-sale and after-sale service.
Consideration	Consideration in contract law, a basic requirement for an enforceable agreement under traditional contract principles, defined in this text as legal value, bargained for and given in exchange for an act or promise. In corporation law, cash or property contributed to a corporation in exchange for shares, or a promise to contribute such cash or property.
Controller	Controller refers to the financial executive primarily responsible for management accounting and financial accounting. Also called chief accounting officer.
Competitor	Other organizations in the same industry or type of business that provide a good or service to the same set of customers is referred to as a competitor.
Market	A market is, as defined in economics, a social arrangement that allows buyers and sellers to discover information and carry out a voluntary exchange of goods or services.
Operation	A standardized method or technique that is performed repetitively, often on different materials resulting in different finished goods is called an operation.
Corporate culture	The whole collection of beliefs, values, and behaviors of a firm that send messages to those within and outside the company about how business is done is the corporate culture.
Decision rule	Decision rule refers to a statement that tells a decision maker which alternative to choose based on the characteristics of the decision situation.
Policy	Similar to a script in that a policy can be a less than completely rational decision-making method. Involves the use of a pre-existing set of decision steps for any problem that presents itself.
Stock	In financial terminology, stock is the capital raized by a corporation, through the issuance and sale of shares.
Purchasing	Purchasing refers to the function in a firm that searches for quality material resources, finds the best suppliers, and negotiates the best price for goods and services.
Asset	An item of property, such as land, capital, money, a share in ownership, or a claim on others for future payment, such as a bond or a bank deposit is an asset.
Firm	An organization that employs resources to produce a good or service for profit and owns and operates one or more plants is referred to as a firm.
Bounded rationality	The understanding that rational decisions are very much bounded or constrained by practical constraints is referred to as bounded rationality.
Satisficing	Satisficing refers to a method for making decisions under bounded rationality; to choose the

first option that meets a set of minimal criteria that have been established.

Small business	Small business refers to a business that is independently owned and operated, is not dominant in its field of operation, and meets certain standards of size in terms of employees or annual receipts.
Agent	A person who makes economic decisions for another economic actor. A hired manager operates as an agent for a firm's owner.
Turnover	Turnover in a financial context refers to the rate at which a provider of goods cycles through its average inventory. Turnover in a human resources context refers to the characteristic of a given company or industry, relative to rate at which an employer gains and loses staff.
Innovation	Innovation refers to the first commercially successful introduction of a new product, the use of a new method of production, or the creation of a new form of business organization.
Points	Loan origination fees that may be deductible as interest by a buyer of property. A seller of property who pays points reduces the selling price by the amount of the points paid for the buyer.
Gain	In finance, gain is a profit or an increase in value of an investment such as a stock or bond. Gain is calculated by fair market value or the proceeds from the sale of the investment minus the sum of the purchase price and all costs associated with it.
Productivity	Productivity refers to the total output of goods and services in a given period of time divided by work hours.
Credit	Credit refers to a recording as positive in the balance of payments, any transaction that gives rise to a payment into the country, such as an export, the sale of an asset, or borrowing from abroad.
Goal displacement	Goal displacement is a phenomenon where following a methodology is more important than the actual developement of a product or service.
Group dynamics	The term group dynamics implies that individual behaviors may differ depending on individuals' current or prospective connections to a sociological group. Group dynamics is the field of study within the social sciences that focuses on the nature of groups. Urges to belong or to identify may make for distinctly different attitudes (recognized or unrecognized), and the influence of a group may rapidly become strong, influencing or overwhelming individual proclivities and actions.
Groupthink	Groupthink is a situation in which pressures for cohesion and togetherness are so strong as to produce narrowly considered and bad decisions; this can be especially true via conformity pressures in groups.
Market share	That fraction of an industry's output accounted for by an individual firm or group of firms is called market share.
Standing	Standing refers to the legal requirement that anyone seeking to challenge a particular action in court must demonstrate that such action substantially affects his legitimate interests before he will be entitled to bring suit.
Production	The creation of finished goods and services using the factors of production: land, labor, capital, entrepreneurship, and knowledge.
Option	A contract that gives the purchaser the option to buy or sell the underlying financial instrument at a specified price, called the exercise price or strike price, within a specific period of time.
Product	Innovations that introduce new goods or services to better meet customer needs are product

innovations	innovations.
Product innovation	The development and sale of a new or improved product is a product innovation. Production of a new product on a commercial basis.
Service	Service refers to a "non tangible product" that is not embodied in a physical good and that typically effects some change in another product, person, or institution. Contrasts with good.
Process innovations	Innovations introducing into operations new and better ways of doing things are called process innovations. Nominations in this category must have made significant achievements in reducing environmental impacts of manufacturing processes, including the acquisition and refinement of materials used by the transportation industries in their products
Process innovation	The development and use of new or improved production or distribution methods is called process innovation. It is an approach in business process reengineering by which radical changes are made through innovations.
Inputs	The inputs used by a firm or an economy are the labor, raw materials, electricity and other resources it uses to produce its outputs.
Premium	Premium refers to the fee charged by an insurance company for an insurance policy. The rate of losses must be relatively predictable: In order to set the premium (prices) insurers must be able to estimate them accurately.
Net income	Net income is equal to the income that a firm has after subtracting costs and expenses from the total revenue. Expenses will typically include tax expense.
Draft	A signed, written order by which one party instructs another party to pay a specified sum to a third party, at sight or at a specific date is a draft.
Preparation	Preparation refers to usually the first stage in the creative process. It includes education and formal training.
Evaluation	The consumer's appraisal of the product or brand on important attributes is called evaluation.
Brainstorming	Brainstorming refers to a technique designed to overcome our natural tendency to evaluate and criticize ideas and thereby reduce the creative output of those ideas. People are encouraged to produce ideas/options without criticizing, often at a very fast pace to minimize our natural tendency to criticize.
Complete information	Complete information refers to the assumption that economic agents know everything that they need to know in order to make optimal decisions. Types of incomplete information are uncertainty and asymmetric information.
Principal	In agency law, one under whose direction an agent acts and for whose benefit that agent acts is a principal.
Delphi Technique	Delphi technique refers to an elaborate attempt to reduce group criticism and increase the generation of good decision options. Ideas are generated in private, anonymously collated and presented to the group.
Best of the best	Term used to refer to outstanding world class benchmark firms is referred to as best of the best.
Decision tree	In decision theory, a decision tree is a graph of decisions and their possible consequences, (including resource costs and risks) used to create a plan to reach a goal.
Advertising campaign	A comprehensive advertising plan that consists of a series of messages in a variety of media that center on a single theme or idea is referred to as an advertising campaign.

Advertising	Advertising refers to paid, nonpersonal communication through various media by organizations and individuals who are in some way identified in the advertising message.
Brief	Brief refers to a statement of a party's case or legal arguments, usually prepared by an attorney. Also used to make legal arguments before appellate courts.
Revenue	Revenue is a U.S. business term for the amount of money that a company receives from its activities, mostly from sales of products and/or services to customers.
Profit	Profit refers to the return to the resource entrepreneurial ability; total revenue minus total cost.
Contract	A contract is a "promise" or an "agreement" that is enforced or recognized by the law. In the civil law, a contract is considered to be part of the general law of obligations.
Capital budgeting	Capital budgeting is the planning process used to determine a firm's long term investments such as new machinery, replacement machinery, new plants, new products, and research and development projects.
Investment	Investment refers to spending for the production and accumulation of capital and additions to inventories. In a financial sense, buying an asset with the expectation of making a return.
Capital	Capital generally refers to financial wealth, especially that used to start or maintain a business. In classical economics, capital is one of four factors of production, the others being land and labor and entrepreneurship.
Payback	A value that indicates the time period required to recoup an initial investment is a payback. The payback does not include the time-value-of-money concept.
Rate of return	A rate of return is a comparison of the money earned (or lost) on an investment to the amount of money invested.
Discounted cash flow	In finance, the discounted cash flow approach describes a method to value a project or an entire company. The DCF methods determine the present value of future cash flows by discounting them using the appropriate cost of capital.
Time value of money	Time value of money is the concept that the value of money varies depending on the timing of the cash flows, given any interest rate greater than zero.
Value of money	Value of money refers to the quantity of goods and services for which a unit of money can be exchanged; the purchasing power of a unit of money; the reciprocal of the price level.
Cash flow	In finance, cash flow refers to the amounts of cash being received and spent by a business during a defined period of time, sometimes tied to a specific project. Most of the time they are being used to determine gaps in the liquid position of a company.
Analyst	Analyst refers to a person or tool with a primary function of information analysis, generally with a more limited, practical and short term set of goals than a researcher.
Balance	In banking and accountancy, the outstanding balance is the amount of money owned, (or due), that remains in a deposit account (or a loan account) at a given date, after all past remittances, payments and withdrawal have been accounted for. It can be positive (then, in the balance sheet of a firm, it is an asset) or negative (a liability).
Optimum	Optimum refers to the best. Usually refers to a most preferred choice by consumers subject to a budget constraint or a profit maximizing choice by firms or industry subject to a technological constraint.
Preventive maintenance	Maintaining scheduled upkeep and improvement to equipment so equipment can actually improve with age is called the preventive maintenance.
Expected value	A representative value from a probability distribution arrived at by multiplying each outcome

Go to **Cram101.com** for the Practice Tests for this Chapter.
And, **NEVER** highlight a book again!

by the associated probability and summing up the values is called the expected value.

Inventory	Tangible property held for sale in the normal course of business or used in producing goods or services for sale is an inventory.
Controlling	A management function that involves determining whether or not an organization is progressing toward its goals and objectives, and taking corrective action if it is not is called controlling.
Escalating commitment	The tendency to continue a previously chosen course of action even when feedback suggests that it is failing is an escalating commitment.
Margin	A deposit by a buyer in stocks with a seller or a stockbroker, as security to cover fluctuations in the market in reference to stocks that the buyer has purchased but for which he has not paid is a margin. Commodities are also traded on margin.
Negotiation	Negotiation is the process whereby interested parties resolve disputes, agree upon courses of action, bargain for individual or collective advantage, and/or attempt to craft outcomes which serve their mutual interests.
Escalation of commitment	Escalation of commitment is the phenomenon where people increase their investment in a decision despite new evidence suggesting that the decision was probably wrong.
Escalation	Regarding the structure of tariffs. In the context of a trade war, escalation refers to the increase in tariffs that occurs as countries retaliate again and again.

Go to **Cram101.com** for the Practice Tests for this Chapter.

Industry	A group of firms that produce identical or similar products is an industry. It is also used specifically to refer to an area of economic production focused on manufacturing which involves large amounts of capital investment before any profit can be realized, also called "heavy industry".
Strategic plan	The formal document that presents the ways and means by which a strategic goal will be achieved is a strategic plan. A long-term flexible plan that does not regulate activities but rather outlines the means to achieve certain results, and provides the means to alter the course of action should the desired ends change.
Mission statement	Mission statement refers to an outline of the fundamental purposes of an organization.
Status quo	Status quo is a Latin term meaning the present, current, existing state of affairs.
Shareware	Software that is copyrighted but distributed to potential customers free of charge is shareware.
Customer satisfaction	Customer satisfaction is a business term which is used to capture the idea of measuring how satisfied an enterprise's customers are with the organization's efforts in a marketplace.
Product development	In business and engineering, new product development is the complete process of bringing a new product to market. There are two parallel aspects to this process : one involves product engineering ; the other marketing analysis. Marketers see new product development as the first stage in product life cycle management, engineers as part of Product Lifecycle Management.
Benchmarking	The continuous process of comparing the levels of performance in producing products and services and executing activities against the best levels of performance is benchmarking.
Effective manager	Leader of a team that consistently achieves high performance goals is an effective manager.
Operational planning	The process of setting work standards and schedules necessary to implement the tactical objectives is operational planning.
Strategic planning	The process of determining the major goals of the organization and the policies and strategies for obtaining and using resources to achieve those goals is called strategic planning.
Management	Management characterizes the process of leading and directing all or part of an organization, often a business, through the deployment and manipulation of resources. Early twentieth-century management writer Mary Parker Follett defined management as "the art of getting things done through people."
Analogy	Analogy is either the cognitive process of transferring information from a particular subject to another particular subject (the target), or a linguistic expression corresponding to such a process. In a narrower sense, analogy is an inference or an argument from a particular to another particular, as opposed to deduction, induction, and abduction, where at least one of the premises or the conclusion is general.
Product line	A group of products that are physically similar or are intended for a similar market are called the product line.
Adidas	Adidas is a German sports apparel manufacturer, part of the Adidas Group. The company was named after its founder, Adolf Dassler, who started producing shoes in the 1920s in Herzogenaurach near Nuremberg with the help of his brother Rudolf Dassler who later formed rival shoe company PUMA AG.
Market	A market is, as defined in economics, a social arrangement that allows buyers and sellers to

Go to **Cram101.com** for the Practice Tests for this Chapter.

discover information and carry out a voluntary exchange of goods or services.

Accounting	A system that collects and processes financial information about an organization and reports that information to decision makers is referred to as accounting.
Marketing	Promoting and selling products or services to customers, or prospective customers, is referred to as marketing.
Foundation	A Foundation is a type of philanthropic organization set up by either individuals or institutions as a legal entity (either as a corporation or trust) with the purpose of distributing grants to support causes in line with the goals of the foundation.
Situation analysis	Taking stock of where the fine or product has been recently, where it is now, and where it is headed in terms of the organization's plans and the external factors and trends affecting it is a situation analysis.
Option	A contract that gives the purchaser the option to buy or sell the underlying financial instrument at a specified price, called the exercise price or strike price, within a specific period of time.
Five competitive forces	There are five competitive forces which can be used to estimate the attractiveness and profitability of entering a business market. They consist of the threat of new entrants, competitive rivalry, the threat of substitute products, the power of buyers, and the power of suppliers
Michael Porter	Michael Porter is a leading contributor to strategic management theory, Porter's main academic objectives focus on how a firm or a region, can build a competitive advantage and develop competitive strategy. Porter's strategic system consists primarily of 5 forces analysis, strategic groups, the value chain, and market positioning stratagies.
Brand	A name, symbol, or design that identifies the goods or services of one seller or group of sellers and distinguishes them from the goods and services of competitors is a brand.
Firm	An organization that employs resources to produce a good or service for profit and owns and operates one or more plants is referred to as a firm.
Competitor	Other organizations in the same industry or type of business that provide a good or service to the same set of customers is referred to as a competitor.
Substitute product	Any product viewed by a consumer as an alternative for other products is a substitute product. The substitution is rarely perfect, and varies from time to time depending on price, availability, etc.
Service	Service refers to a "non tangible product" that is not embodied in a physical good and that typically effects some change in another product, person, or institution. Contrasts with good.
Bargaining power	Bargaining power refers to the ability to influence the setting of prices or wages, usually arising from some sort of monopoly or monopsony position
Nike	Because Nike creates goods for a wide range of sports, they have competition from every sports and sports fashion brand there is. Nike has no direct competitors because there is no single brand which can compete directly with their range of sports and non-sports oriented gear, except for Reebok.
Wage	The payment for the service of a unit of labor, per unit time. In trade theory, it is the only payment to labor, usually unskilled labor. In empirical work, wage data may exclude other compenzation, which must be added to get the total cost of employment.
Buyer	A buyer refers to a role in the buying center with formal authority and responsibility to select the supplier and negotiate the terms of the contract.

Business strategy	Business strategy, which refers to the aggregated operational strategies of single business firm or that of an SBU in a diversified corporation refers to the way in which a firm competes in its chosen arenas.
Critical success factor	Critical Success Factor is a business term for an element which is necessary for an organization or project to achieve its mission.
Success factor	The term success factor refers to the characteristics necessary for high performance; knowledge, skills, abilities, behaviors.
Assessment	Collecting information and providing feedback to employees about their behavior, communication style, or skills is an assessment.
Customer value	Customer value refers to the unique combination of benefits received by targeted buyers that includes quality, price, convenience, on-time delivery, and both before-sale and after-sale service.
Inventory control	Inventory control, in the field of loss prevention, are systems designed to introduce technical barriers to shoplifting.
Inventory	Tangible property held for sale in the normal course of business or used in producing goods or services for sale is an inventory.
Slowdown	A slowdown is an industrial action in which employees perform their duties but seek to reduce productivity or efficiency in their performance of these duties. A slowdown may be used as either a prelude or an alternative to a strike, as it is seen as less disruptive as well as less risky and costly for workers and their union.
Contract	A contract is a "promise" or an "agreement" that is enforced or recognized by the law. In the civil law, a contract is considered to be part of the general law of obligations.
Public relations	Public relations refers to the management function that evaluates public attitudes, changes policies and procedures in response to the public's requests, and executes a program of action and information to earn public understanding and acceptance.
Sweatshop	A sweatshop is a factory or workshop that has attributes in common with the workplaces of the pejoratively-named sweating system of the 1840s. Sweatshops arose at a time when workers did not have the protections afforded by trade unions or labor laws, and sweatshops are synonymous with working conditions that violate human rights sensibilities and sometimes public policies. .
SWOT	SWOT analysis refers to an acronym describing an organization's appraisal of its internal strengths and weaknesses and its external opportunities and threats.
Competitive advantage	A business is said to have a competitive advantage when its unique strengths, often based on cost, quality, time, and innovation, offer consumers a greater percieved value and there by differtiating it from its competitors.
Logo	Logo refers to device or other brand name that cannot be spoken.
Technology	The body of knowledge and techniques that can be used to combine economic resources to produce goods and services is called technology.
Sustainable competitive advantage	A strength, relative to competitors, in the markets served and the products offered is referred to as the sustainable competitive advantage.
Core competency	A company's core competency are things that a firm can (alsosns) do well and that meet the following three conditions. 1. It provides customer benefits, 2. It is hard for competitors to imitate, and 3. it can be leveraged widely to many products and market. A core competency can take various forms, including technical/subject matter knowhow, a reliable process,

Go to **Cram101.com** for the Practice Tests for this Chapter.
And, **NEVER** highlight a book again!

and/or close relationships with customers and suppliers. It may also include product development or culture such as employee dedication. Modern business theories suggest that most activities that are not part of a company's core competency should be outsourced.

Core | A core is the set of feasible allocations in an economy that cannot be improved upon by subset of the set of the economy's consumers (a coalition). In construction, when the force in an element is within a certain center section, the core, the element will only be under compression.

Wall Street Journal | Dow Jones & Company was founded in 1882 by reporters Charles Dow, Edward Jones and Charles Bergstresser. Jones converted the small Customers' Afternoon Letter into The Wall Street Journal, first published in 1889, and began delivery of the Dow Jones News Service via telegraph. The Journal featured the Jones 'Average', the first of several indexes of stock and bond prices on the New York Stock Exchange.

Journal | Book of original entry, in which transactions are recorded in a general ledger system, is referred to as a journal.

Fiscal year | A fiscal year is a 12-month period used for calculating annual ("yearly") financial reports in businesses and other organizations. In many jurisdictions, regulatory laws regarding accounting require such reports once per twelve months, but do not require that the twelve months constitute a calendar year (i.e. January to December).

Market share | That fraction of an industry's output accounted for by an individual firm or group of firms is called market share.

Net profit | Net profit is an accounting term which is commonly used in business. It is equal to the gross revenue for a given time period minus associated expenses.

Profit | Profit refers to the return to the resource entrepreneurial ability; total revenue minus total cost.

International Business | International business refers to any firm that engages in international trade or investment.

Evaluation | The consumer's appraisal of the product or brand on important attributes is called evaluation.

Frequency | Frequency refers to the speed of the up and down movements of a fluctuating economic variable; that is, the number of times per unit of time that the variable completes a cycle of up and down movement.

Promotion | Promotion refers to all the techniques sellers use to motivate people to buy products or services. An attempt by marketers to inform people about products and to persuade them to participate in an exchange.

Corporate Strategy | Corporate strategy is concerned with the firm's choice of business, markets and activities and thus it defines the overall scope and direction of the business.

Retrenchment | Retrenchment means the reduction of expenditures in order to become financially stable. It is a tactical concept similar to downsizing.

Growth strategy | A strategy based on investing in companies and sectors which are growing faster than their peers is a growth strategy. The benefits are usually in the form of capital gains rather than dividends.

Stability strategy | When organizations are satisfied with their current rate of growth and profits, they may decide to use a stability strategy. This strategy is essentially a continuation of existing strategies.

Turnaround | A strategy to reverse a firms failing business is a turnaround strategy.

strategy	
Liquidation	Liquidation refers to a process whereby the assets of a business are converted to money. The conversion may be coerced by a legal process to pay off the debt of the business, or to satisfy any other business obligation that the business has not voluntarily satisfied.
Divestiture	In finance and economics, divestiture is the reduction of some kind of asset, for either financial or social goals. A divestment is the opposite of an investment.
Asset	An item of property, such as land, capital, money, a share in ownership, or a claim on others for future payment, such as a bond or a bank deposit is an asset.
Decreasing cost	Average cost that declines as output increases, due to increasing returns to scale is called decreasing cost.
Cash flow	In finance, cash flow refers to the amounts of cash being received and spent by a business during a defined period of time, sometimes tied to a specific project. Most of the time they are being used to determine gaps in the liquid position of a company.
Revenue	Revenue is a U.S. business term for the amount of money that a company receives from its activities, mostly from sales of products and/or services to customers.
Converse	Converse is an American shoe company which has been making shoes since the early 20th century. The company's main turning point came in 1917 when the Converse All-Star basketball shoe was introduced. This was a real innovation at the time, considering the sport was only 25 years old.
Chapter 11 bankruptcy	Chapter 11 bankruptcy governs the process of reorganization under the bankruptcy laws of the United States. It is an attempt to stay in business while a bankruptcy court supervises the "reorganization" of the company's contractual and debt obligations.
Acquisition	A company's purchase of the property and obligations of another company is an acquisition.
Bankruptcy	Bankruptcy is a legally declared inability or impairment of ability of an individual or organization to pay their creditors.
Operation	A standardized method or technique that is performed repetitively, often on different materials resulting in different finished goods is called an operation.
Corporation	A legal entity chartered by a state or the Federal government that is distinct and separate from the individuals who own it is a corporation. This separation gives the corporation unique powers which other legal entities lack.
Unrelated diversification	A business strategy in which an organization operates several businesses that are not associated with one another is unrelated diversification.
Forward integration	Practice in corporate vertical marketing system in which a producer also owns retail shops is a forward integration.
Diversification	Investing in a collection of assets whose returns do not always move together, with the result that overall risk is lower than for individual assets is referred to as diversification.
Integration	Economic integration refers to reducing barriers among countries to transactions and to movements of goods, capital, and labor, including harmonization of laws, regulations, and standards. Integrated markets theoretically function as a unified market.
Concentration strategy	A strategy focusing on increasing market share, reducing costs, or creating and maintaining a market niche for products and a service is called concentration strategy.
Backward integration	A form of vertical integration that involves the purchase of suppliers in order to reduce dependency is backward integration.

Television network	Television network refers to the provider of news and programming to a series of affiliated local television stations.
Diversification strategy	Diversification strategy is a corporate strategy that takes the organization away from both its current markets and products, as opposed to either market or product development.
Merger	Merger refers to the combination of two firms into a single firm.
Mergers and acquisitions	The phrase mergers and acquisitions refers to the aspect of corporate finance strategy and management dealing with the merging and acquiring of different companies as well as other assets. Usually mergers occur in a friendly setting where executives from the respective companies participate in a due diligence process to ensure a successful combination of all parts.
Economy	The income, expenditures, and resources that affect the cost of running a business and household are called an economy.
Expense	In accounting, an expense represents an event in which an asset is used up or a liability is incurred. In terms of the accounting equation, expenses reduce owners' equity.
Shareholder	A shareholder is an individual or company (including a corporation) that legally owns one or more shares of stock in a joined stock company.
Purchasing	Purchasing refers to the function in a firm that searches for quality material resources, finds the best suppliers, and negotiates the best price for goods and services.
Takeover	A takeover in business refers to one company (the acquirer) purchasing another (the target). Such events resemble mergers, but without the formation of a new company.
Bid	A bid price is a price offered by a buyer when he/she buys a good. In the context of stock trading on a stock exchange, the bid price is the highest price a buyer of a stock is willing to pay for a share of that given stock.
Portfolio	In finance, a portfolio is a collection of investments held by an institution or a private individual. Holding but not always a portfolio is part of an investment and risk-limiting strategy called diversification. By owning several assets, certain types of risk (in particular specific risk) can be reduced.
Allocate	Allocate refers to the assignment of income for various tax purposes. A multistate corporation's nonbusiness income usually is distributed to the state where the nonbusiness assets are located; it is not apportioned with the rest of the entity's income.
Subsidiary	A company that is controlled by another company or corporation is a subsidiary.
Bcg matrix	A concept developed by the Boston Consulting Group that evaluates strategic business units with respect to the dimensions of business growth rate and market share is a bcg matrix.
Boston Consulting Group	The Boston Consulting Group is a management consulting firm founded by Harvard Business School alum Bruce Henderson in 1963. In 1965 Bruce Henderson thought that to survive, much less grow, in a competitive landscape occupied by hundreds of larger and better-known consulting firms, a distinctive identity was needed, and pioneered "Business Strategy" as a special area of expertise.
Cash cow	A cash cow is a product or a business unit that generates unusually high profit margins: so high that it is responsible for a large amount of a company's operating profit.
Innovation	Innovation refers to the first commercially successful introduction of a new product, the use of a new method of production, or the creation of a new form of business organization.
Competitive Strategy	An outline of how a business intends to compete with other firms in the same industry is called competitive strategy.

Cost leadership	Organization's ability to achieve lower costs relative to competitors through productivity and efficiency improvements, elimination of waste, and tight cost control is cost leadership.
Leadership	Management merely consists of leadership applied to business situations; or in other words: management forms a sub-set of the broader process of leadership.
Product differentiation	A strategy in which one firm's product is distinguished from competing products by means of its design, related services, quality, location, or other attributes is called product differentiation.
Cost Leadership Strategy	Using a serious commitment to reducing expenses that, in turn, lowers the price of the items sold in a relatively broad array of market segments is called cost leadership strategy.
Market niche	A market niche or niche market is a focused, targetable portion of a market. By definition, then, a business that focuses on a niche market is addressing a need for a product or service that is not being addressed by mainstream providers.
Niche	In industry, a niche is a situation or an activity perfectly suited to a person. A niche can imply a working position or an area suited to a person who occupies it. Basically, a job where a person is able to succeed and thrive.
Loyalty	Marketers tend to define customer loyalty as making repeat purchases. Some argue that it should be defined attitudinally as a strongly positive feeling about the brand.
Gain	In finance, gain is a profit or an increase in value of an investment such as a stock or bond. Gain is calculated by fair market value or the proceeds from the sale of the investment minus the sum of the purchase price and all costs associated with it.
Pricing strategy	The process in which the price of a product can be determined and is decided upon is a pricing strategy.
Production	The creation of finished goods and services using the factors of production: land, labor, capital, entrepreneurship, and knowledge.
Advertising	Advertising refers to paid, nonpersonal communication through various media by organizations and individuals who are in some way identified in the advertising message.
Interest	In finance and economics, interest is the price paid by a borrower for the use of a lender's money. In other words, interest is the amount of paid to "rent" money for a period of time.
Growth stage	The second stage of the product life cycle characterized by rapid increases in sales and by the appearance of competitors is referred to as the growth stage.
Maturity	Maturity refers to the final payment date of a loan or other financial instrument, after which point no further interest or principal need be paid.
Product life cycle	Product life cycle refers to a series of phases in a product's sales and cash flows over time; these phases, in order of occurrence, are introductory, growth, maturity, and decline.
Operational strategy	The "lowest" level of strategy is operational strategy. It is very narrow in focus and deals with day-to-day operational activities such as scheduling criteria. It must operate within a budget but is not at liberty to adjust or create that budget.
Human resources	Human resources refers to the individuals within the firm, and to the portion of the firm's organization that deals with hiring, firing, training, and other personnel issues.
Brief	Brief refers to a statement of a party's case or legal arguments, usually prepared by an attorney. Also used to make legal arguments before appellate courts.
Target market	One or more specific groups of potential consumers toward which an organization directs its marketing program are a target market.

Balance	In banking and accountancy, the outstanding balance is the amount of money owned, (or due), that remains in a deposit account (or a loan account) at a given date, after all past remittances, payments and withdrawal have been accounted for. It can be positive (then, in the balance sheet of a firm, it is an asset) or negative (a liability).
Inputs	The inputs used by a firm or an economy are the labor, raw materials, electricity and other resources it uses to produce its outputs.
Empowerment	Giving employees the authority and responsibility to respond quickly to customer requests is called empowerment.
Income statement	Income statement refers to a financial statement that presents the revenues and expenses and resulting net income or net loss of a company for a specific period of time.
Balance sheet	A statement of the assets, liabilities, and net worth of a firm or individual at some given time often at the end of its "fiscal year," is referred to as a balance sheet.
Dividend	Amount of corporate profits paid out for each share of stock is referred to as dividend.
Budget	Budget refers to an account, usually for a year, of the planned expenditures and the expected receipts of an entity. For a government, the receipts are tax revenues.
Equity	Equity is the name given to the set of legal principles, in countries following the English common law tradition, which supplement strict rules of law where their application would operate harshly, so as to achieve what is sometimes referred to as "natural justice."
Stock	In financial terminology, stock is the capital raized by a corporation, through the issuance and sale of shares.
Research and development	The use of resources for the deliberate discovery of new information and ways of doing things, together with the application of that information in inventing new products or processes is referred to as research and development.
Controlling	A management function that involves determining whether or not an organization is progressing toward its goals and objectives, and taking corrective action if it is not is called controlling.
Functional manager	A manager who is responsible for a department that performs a single functional task and has employees with similar training and skills is referred to as a functional manager.
Corporate level	Corporate level refers to level at which top management directs overall strategy for the entire organization.
Management by objectives	Management by objectives is a process of agreeing upon objectives within an organization so that management and employees buy in to the objectives and understand what they are.
SWOT analysis	SWOT analysis refers to an acronym describing an organization's appraisal of its internal strengths and weaknesses and its external opportunities and threats.
Internal environment	Variables that are under some degree of control by organizational members is the internal enviroment. Internal environment scans are conducted to identify an organization's internal capabilities, performance levels, strengths, and weaknesses.
Disney	Disney is one of the largest media and entertainment corporations in the world. Founded on October 16, 1923 by brothers Walt and Roy Disney as a small animation studio, today it is one of the largest Hollywood studios and also owns nine theme parks and several television networks, including the American Broadcasting Company (ABC).
Distribution	Distribution in economics, the manner in which total output and income is distributed among individuals or factors.
Boot	Boot is any type of personal property received in a real property transaction that is not

like kind, such as cash, mortgage notes, a boat or stock. The exchanger pays taxes on the boot to the extent of recognized capital gain. In an exchange if any funds are not used in purchasing the replacement property, that also will be called boot.

Dealer	People who link buyers with sellers by buying and selling securities at stated prices are referred to as a dealer.
Information system	An information system is a system whether automated or manual, that comprises people, machines, and/or methods organized to collect, process, transmit, and disseminate data that represent user information.
Preparation	Preparation refers to usually the first stage in the creative process. It includes education and formal training.
Mistake	In contract law a mistake is incorrect understanding by one or more parties to a contract and may be used as grounds to invalidate the agreement. Common law has identified three different types of mistake in contract: unilateral mistake, mutual mistake, and common mistake.
Entrepreneur	The owner/operator. The person who organizes, manages, and assumes the risks of a firm, taking a new idea or a new product and turning it into a successful business is an entrepreneur.
Aid	Assistance provided by countries and by international institutions such as the World Bank to developing countries in the form of monetary grants, loans at low interest rates, in kind, or a combination of these is called aid. Aid can also refer to assistance of any type rendered to benefit some group or individual.
Commerce	Commerce is the exchange of something of value between two entities. It is the central mechanism from which capitalism is derived.

Standing plan	An ongoing plan used to provide guidance for tasks performed repeatedly within the organization is a standing plan.
Standing	Standing refers to the legal requirement that anyone seeking to challenge a particular action in court must demonstrate that such action substantially affects his legitimate interests before he will be entitled to bring suit.
Jury	A body of lay persons, selected by lot, or by some other fair and impartial means, to ascertain, under the guidance of the judge, the truth in questions of fact arising either in civil litigation or a criminal process is referred to as jury.
Time series	In statistics and signal processing, a time series is a sequence of data points, measured typically at successive times, spaced at (often uniform) time intervals. Analysts throughout the economy will use these to aid in the management of their corresponding businesses.
Gantt chart	Bar graph showing production managers what projects are being worked on and what stage they are in at any given time is a gantt chart.
Management	Management characterizes the process of leading and directing all or part of an organization, often a business, through the deployment and manipulation of resources. Early twentieth-century management writer Mary Parker Follett defined management as "the art of getting things done through people."
Strategic planning	The process of determining the major goals of the organization and the policies and strategies for obtaining and using resources to achieve those goals is called strategic planning.
Revenue	Revenue is a U.S. business term for the amount of money that a company receives from its activities, mostly from sales of products and/or services to customers.
Committee	A long-lasting, sometimes permanent team in the organization structure created to deal with tasks that recur regularly is the committee.
Competitive bidding	A situation where two or more companies submit bids for a product, service, or project to a potential buyer is competitive bidding.
Facility management	In business, facility management is the management of buildings and services. It is the role of facility management to ensure that everything is available for the other staff in an organization to do their work.
Brand	A name, symbol, or design that identifies the goods or services of one seller or group of sellers and distinguishes them from the goods and services of competitors is a brand.
Interest	In finance and economics, interest is the price paid by a borrower for the use of a lender's money. In other words, interest is the amount of paid to "rent" money for a period of time.
Operation	A standardized method or technique that is performed repetitively, often on different materials resulting in different finished goods is called an operation.
Authority	Authority in agency law, refers to an agent's ability to affect his principal's legal relations with third parties. Also used to refer to an actor's legal power or ability to do something. In addition, sometimes used to refer to a statute, case, or other legal source that justifies a particular result.
Budget	Budget refers to an account, usually for a year, of the planned expenditures and the expected receipts of an entity. For a government, the receipts are tax revenues.
Franchise	A contractual right to sell certain products or services, use certain trademarks, or perform activities in a geographical region is called a franchise.
Firm	An organization that employs resources to produce a good or service for profit and owns and

operates one or more plants is referred to as a firm.

Contract	A contract is a "promise" or an "agreement" that is enforced or recognized by the law. In the civil law, a contract is considered to be part of the general law of obligations.
Service	Service refers to a "non tangible product" that is not embodied in a physical good and that typically effects some change in another product, person, or institution. Contrasts with good.
Industry	A group of firms that produce identical or similar products is an industry. It is also used specifically to refer to an area of economic production focused on manufacturing which involves large amounts of capital investment before any profit can be realized, also called "heavy industry".
Concession	A concession is a business operated under a contract or license associated with a degree of exclusivity in exploiting a business within a certain geographical area. For example, sports arenas or public parks may have concession stands; and public services such as water supply may be operated as concessions.
Security	Security refers to a claim on the borrower future income that is sold by the borrower to the lender. A security is a type of transferable interest representing financial value.
Appeal	Appeal refers to the act of asking an appellate court to overturn a decision after the trial court's final judgment has been entered.
Venue	A requirement distinct from jurisdiction that the court be geographically situated so that it is the most appropriate and convenient court to try the case is the venue.
Policy	Similar to a script in that a policy can be a less than completely rational decision-making method. Involves the use of a pre-existing set of decision steps for any problem that presents itself.
Union	A worker association that bargains with employers over wages and working conditions is called a union.
Labor union	A group of workers organized to advance the interests of the group is called a labor union.
Labor	People's physical and mental talents and efforts that are used to help produce goods and services are called labor.
Due process	Due process of law is a legal concept that ensures the government will respect all of a person's legal rights instead of just some or most of those legal rights when the government deprives a person of life, liberty, or property.
Grievance	A charge by employees that management is not abiding by the terms of the negotiated labormanagement agreement is the grievance.
General manager	A manager who is responsible for several departments that perform different functions is called general manager.
Accounting	A system that collects and processes financial information about an organization and reports that information to decision makers is referred to as accounting.
Production	The creation of finished goods and services using the factors of production: land, labor, capital, entrepreneurship, and knowledge.
Personnel	A collective term for all of the employees of an organization. Personnel is also commonly used to refer to the personnel management function or the organizational unit responsible for administering personnel programs.
Purchasing	Purchasing refers to the function in a firm that searches for quality material resources, finds the best suppliers, and negotiates the best price for goods and services.

Go to **Cram101.com** for the Practice Tests for this Chapter.

Inventory	Tangible property held for sale in the normal course of business or used in producing goods or services for sale is an inventory.
Effective manager	Leader of a team that consistently achieves high performance goals is an effective manager.
Overtime	Overtime is the amount of time someone works beyond normal working hours.
Physical resources	Natural resources used in the transformation process to create resources of more value are called physical resources.
Sales forecasting	Sales forecasting refers to the process of predicting sales of services or goods. The initial step in preparing a master budget.
Sales forecast	Sales forecast refers to the maximum total sales of a product that a firm expects to sell during a specified time period under specified environmental conditions and its own marketing efforts.
Staffing	Staffing refers to a management function that includes hiring, motivating, and retaining the best people available to accomplish the company's objectives.
Supply	Supply is the aggregate amount of any material good that can be called into being at a certain price point; it comprises one half of the equation of supply and demand. In classical economic theory, a curve representing supply is one of the factors that produce price.
Marketing	Promoting and selling products or services to customers, or prospective customers, is referred to as marketing.
Expense	In accounting, an expense represents an event in which an asset is used up or a liability is incurred. In terms of the accounting equation, expenses reduce owners' equity.
Human resources	Human resources refers to the individuals within the firm, and to the portion of the firm's organization that deals with hiring, firing, training, and other personnel issues.
Layoff	A layoff is the termination of an employee or (more commonly) a group of employees for business reasons, such as the decision that certain positions are no longer necessary.
Market share	That fraction of an industry's output accounted for by an individual firm or group of firms is called market share.
Market	A market is, as defined in economics, a social arrangement that allows buyers and sellers to discover information and carry out a voluntary exchange of goods or services.
Corporation	A legal entity chartered by a state or the Federal government that is distinct and separate from the individuals who own it is a corporation. This separation gives the corporation unique powers which other legal entities lack.
Bankruptcy	Bankruptcy is a legally declared inability or impairment of ability of an individual or organization to pay their creditors.
Economy	The income, expenditures, and resources that affect the cost of running a business and household are called an economy.
Option	A contract that gives the purchaser the option to buy or sell the underlying financial instrument at a specified price, called the exercise price or strike price, within a specific period of time.
Nike	Because Nike creates goods for a wide range of sports, they have competition from every sports and sports fashion brand there is. Nike has no direct competitors because there is no single brand which can compete directly with their range of sports and non-sports oriented gear, except for Reebok.

Go to **Cram101.com** for the Practice Tests for this Chapter.

Adidas	Adidas is a German sports apparel manufacturer, part of the Adidas Group. The company was named after its founder, Adolf Dassler, who started producing shoes in the 1920s in Herzogenaurach near Nuremberg with the help of his brother Rudolf Dassler who later formed rival shoe company PUMA AG.
Hosting	Internet hosting service is a service that runs Internet servers, allowing organizations and individuals to serve content on the Internet.
Trend	Trend refers to the long-term movement of an economic variable, such as its average rate of increase or decrease over enough years to encompass several business cycles.
Regression analysis	Regression analysis refers to the statistical technique of finding a straight line that approximates the information in a group of data points. Used throughout empirical economics, including both international trade and finance.
Simple regression	Regression model that estimates the relationship between a dependent variable and one independent variable is referred to as simple regression.
Carrying costs	Carrying costs refers to costs that arise while holding an inventory of goods for sale.
Carrying cost	The cost to hold an asset, usually inventory is called a carrying cost. For inventory, a carrying cost includes such items as interest, warehousing costs, insurance, and material-handling expenses.
Nonprofit organization	An organization whose goals do not include making a personal profit for its owners is a nonprofit organization.
Interdependence	The extent to which departments depend on each other for resources or materials to accomplish their tasks is referred to as interdependence.
Evaluation	The consumer's appraisal of the product or brand on important attributes is called evaluation.
Critical path	The sequence of tasks that limit how quickly a project can be completed is referred to as critical path.
Stock	In financial terminology, stock is the capital raized by a corporation, through the issuance and sale of shares.
Time management	Time Management refers to tools or techniques for planning and scheduling time, usually with the aim to increase the effectiveness and/or efficiency of personal and corporate time use.
Competitive advantage	A business is said to have a competitive advantage when its unique strengths, often based on cost, quality, time, and innovation, offer consumers a greater percieved value and there by differtiating it from its competitors.
Productivity	Productivity refers to the total output of goods and services in a given period of time divided by work hours.
Financial management	The job of managing a firm's resources so it can meet its goals and objectives is called financial management.
Leadership	Management merely consists of leadership applied to business situations; or in other words: management forms a sub-set of the broader process of leadership.
Management system	A management system is the framework of processes and procedures used to ensure that an organization can fulfill all tasks required to achieve its objectives.
Context	The effect of the background under which a message often takes on more and richer meaning is a context. Context is especially important in cross-cultural interactions because some cultures are said to be high context or low context.

Go to **Cram101.com** for the Practice Tests for this Chapter.

Balance	In banking and accountancy, the outstanding balance is the amount of money owned, (or due), that remains in a deposit account (or a loan account) at a given date, after all past remittances, payments and withdrawal have been accounted for. It can be positive (then, in the balance sheet of a firm, it is an asset) or negative (a liability).
Controlling	A management function that involves determining whether or not an organization is progressing toward its goals and objectives, and taking corrective action if it is not is called controlling.
Contingency planning	The process of preparing alternative courses of action that may be used if the primary plans do not achieve the objectives of the organization is called contingency planning.
Assessment	Collecting information and providing feedback to employees about their behavior, communication style, or skills is an assessment.
Forming	The first stage of team development, where the team is formed and the objectives for the team are set is referred to as forming.
Slowdown	A slowdown is an industrial action in which employees perform their duties but seek to reduce productivity or efficiency in their performance of these duties. A slowdown may be used as either a prelude or an alternative to a strike, as it is seen as less disruptive as well as less risky and costly for workers and their union.
Cash cow	A cash cow is a product or a business unit that generates unusually high profit margins: so high that it is responsible for a large amount of a company's operating profit.
Fund	Independent accounting entity with a self-balancing set of accounts segregated for the purposes of carrying on specific activities is referred to as a fund.
Margin	A deposit by a buyer in stocks with a seller or a stockbroker, as security to cover fluctuations in the market in reference to stocks that the buyer has purchased but for which he has not paid is a margin. Commodities are also traded on margin.
Gain	In finance, gain is a profit or an increase in value of an investment such as a stock or bond. Gain is calculated by fair market value or the proceeds from the sale of the investment minus the sum of the purchase price and all costs associated with it.
Profit	Profit refers to the return to the resource entrepreneurial ability; total revenue minus total cost.
Financial plan	The financial plan section of a business plan consists of three financial statements (the income statement, the cash flow projection, and the balance sheet) and a brief analysis of these three statements.
Profit center	Responsibility center where the manager is accountable for revenues and costs is referred to as a profit center.
Preparation	Preparation refers to usually the first stage in the creative process. It includes education and formal training.
Fixture	Fixture refers to a thing that was originally personal property and that has been actually or constructively affixed to the soil itself or to some structure legally a part of the land.
Lease	A contract for the possession and use of land or other property, including goods, on one side, and a recompense of rent or other income on the other is the lease.
Credit	Credit refers to a recording as positive in the balance of payments, any transaction that gives rise to a payment into the country, such as an export, the sale of an asset, or borrowing from abroad.

Preparation	Preparation refers to usually the first stage in the creative process. It includes education and formal training.
Liaison	An individual who serves as a bridge between groups, tying groups together and facilitating the communication flow needed to integrate group activities is a liaison.
Authority	Authority in agency law, refers to an agent's ability to affect his principal's legal relations with third parties. Also used to refer to an actor's legal power or ability to do something. In addition, sometimes used to refer to a statute, case, or other legal source that justifies a particular result.
Departmental-zation	The dividing of organizational functions into separate units is called departmentalization.
Job simplification	Job simplification involves breaking complex jobs down into a sequence of specialized tasks to be conducted by different employees, resulting in clearly defined jobs characterized by limited skill requirements and little autonomy or responsibility.
Job Characteristics Model	A conceptual framework for designing motivating jobs that create meaningful work experiences that satisfy employees' growth needs is referred to as the job characteristics model.
Resource allocator	A resource allocator is a plan for using available resources, for example human resources, especially in the near term, to achieve goals for the future. It is the process of allocating resources among the various projects or business units.
Effective manager	Leader of a team that consistently achieves high performance goals is an effective manager.
Management	Management characterizes the process of leading and directing all or part of an organization, often a business, through the deployment and manipulation of resources. Early twentieth-century management writer Mary Parker Follett defined management as "the art of getting things done through people."
Chain of command	An unbroken line of authority that links all individuals in the organization and specifies who reports to whom is a chain of command. The concept of chain of command also implies that higher rank alone does not entitle a person to give commands.
Span of control	Span of control refers to the optimum number of subordinates a manager supervises or should supervise.
Flat organization	Flat organization refers to a organizational structure with few or no levels of intervening management between staff and managers. The idea is that well-trained workers will be more productive when they are more directly involved in the decision making process, rather than closely supervised by many layers of management.
Hierarchy	A system of grouping people in an organization according to rank from the top down in which all subordinate managers must report to one person is called a hierarchy.
Competitive advantage	A business is said to have a competitive advantage when its unique strengths, often based on cost, quality, time, and innovation, offer consumers a greater percieved value and there by diffentiating it from its competitors.
Gain	In finance, gain is a profit or an increase in value of an investment such as a stock or bond. Gain is calculated by fair market value or the proceeds from the sale of the investment minus the sum of the purchase price and all costs associated with it.
Customer value	Customer value refers to the unique combination of benefits received by targeted buyers that includes quality, price, convenience, on-time delivery, and both before-sale and after-sale service.

Go to **Cram101.com** for the Practice Tests for this Chapter.

Operation	A standardized method or technique that is performed repetitively, often on different materials resulting in different finished goods is called an operation.
Pay for Performance	A one-time cash payment to an investment center manager as a reward for meeting a predetermined criterion on a specified performance measure is referred to as pay for performance.
Business model	A business model is the instrument by which a business intends to generate revenue and profits. It is a summary of how a company means to serve its employees and customers, and involves both strategy (what an business intends to do) as well as an implementation.
Bureaucracy	Bureaucracy refers to an organization with many layers of managers who set rules and regulations and oversee all decisions.
Integration	Economic integration refers to reducing barriers among countries to transactions and to movements of goods, capital, and labor, including harmonization of laws, regulations, and standards. Integrated markets theoretically function as a unified market.
Committee	A long-lasting, sometimes permanent team in the organization structure created to deal with tasks that recur regularly is the committee.
Project manager	Project manager refers to a manager responsible for a temporary work project that involves the participation of other people from various functions and levels of the organization.
Customer service	The ability of logistics management to satisfy users in terms of time, dependability, communication, and convenience is called the customer service.
Public relations	Public relations refers to the management function that evaluates public attitudes, changes policies and procedures in response to the public's requests, and executes a program of action and information to earn public understanding and acceptance.
Purchasing	Purchasing refers to the function in a firm that searches for quality material resources, finds the best suppliers, and negotiates the best price for goods and services.
Service	Service refers to a "non tangible product" that is not embodied in a physical good and that typically effects some change in another product, person, or institution. Contrasts with good.
Security	Security refers to a claim on the borrower future income that is sold by the borrower to the lender. A security is a type of transferable interest representing financial value.
Closing	The finalization of a real estate sales transaction that passes title to the property from the seller to the buyer is referred to as a closing. Closing is a sales term which refers to the process of making a sale. It refers to reaching the final step, which may be an exchange of money or acquiring a signature.
Venue	A requirement distinct from jurisdiction that the court be geographically situated so that it is the most appropriate and convenient court to try the case is the venue.
Federal government	Federal government refers to the government of the United States, as distinct from the state and local governments.
Evaluation	The consumer's appraisal of the product or brand on important attributes is called evaluation.
Delegation	Delegation is the handing of a task over to another person, usually a subordinate. It is the assignment of authority and responsibility to another person to carry out specific activities.
Customer satisfaction	Customer satisfaction is a business term which is used to capture the idea of measuring how satisfied an enterprise's customers are with the organization's efforts in a marketplace.

Organization chart	Organization chart refers to a visual device, which shows the relationship and divides the organization's work; it shows who is accountable for the completion of specific work and who reports to whom.
Trust	An arrangement in which shareholders of independent firms agree to give up their stock in exchange for trust certificates that entitle them to a share of the trust's common profits.
Leadership	Management merely consists of leadership applied to business situations; or in other words: management forms a sub-set of the broader process of leadership.
Scope	Scope of a project is the sum total of all projects products and their requirements or features.
Supervisor	A Supervisor is an employee of an organization with some of the powers and responsibilities of management, occupying a role between true manager and a regular employee. A Supervisor position is typically the first step towards being promoted into a management role.
Line authority	A form of authority in which individuals in management positions have the formal power to direct and control immediate subordinates is referred to as line authority.
Marketing	Promoting and selling products or services to customers, or prospective customers, is referred to as marketing.
Personnel	A collective term for all of the employees of an organization. Personnel is also commonly used to refer to the personnel management function or the organizational unit responsible for administering personnel programs.
Human resources	Human resources refers to the individuals within the firm, and to the portion of the firm's organization that deals with hiring, firing, training, and other personnel issues.
Data processing	Data processing refers to a name for business technology in the 1970s; included technology that supported an existing business and was primarily used to improve the flow of financial information.
Internal customer	An individuals or unit within the firm that receives services from other entities within the organization is an internal customer.
Line personnel	Employees who perform functions that contribute directly to the primary goals of the organization are called line personnel.
Specialist	A specialist is a trader who makes a market in one or several stocks and holds the limit order book for those stocks.
Accounting	A system that collects and processes financial information about an organization and reports that information to decision makers is referred to as accounting.
Centralized authority	An organization structure in which decision-making authority is maintained at the top level of management at the company's headquarters is a centralized authority.
Balance	In banking and accountancy, the outstanding balance is the amount of money owned, (or due), that remains in a deposit account (or a loan account) at a given date, after all past remittances, payments and withdrawal have been accounted for. It can be positive (then, in the balance sheet of a firm, it is an asset) or negative (a liability).
Organizational design	The structuring of workers so that they can best accomplish the firm's goals is referred to as organizational design.
Firm	An organization that employs resources to produce a good or service for profit and owns and operates one or more plants is referred to as a firm.
Informal organization	Informal organization refers to the system of relationships and lines of authority that develops spontaneously as employees meet and form power centers; that is, the human side of

the organization that does not appear on any organization chart.

Administration	Administration refers to the management and direction of the affairs of governments and institutions; a collective term for all policymaking officials of a government; the execution and implementation of public policy.
Licensing	Licensing is a form of strategic alliance which involves the sale of a right to use certain proprietary knowledge (so called intellectual property) in a defined way.
Staff position	A manager in a staff position has the authority and responsibility to advise people in the line positions but cannot issue direct orders to them.
Production	The creation of finished goods and services using the factors of production: land, labor, capital, entrepreneurship, and knowledge.
Warrant	A warrant is a security that entitles the holder to buy or sell a certain additional quantity of an underlying security at an agreed-upon price, at the holder's discretion.
Nike	Because Nike creates goods for a wide range of sports, they have competition from every sports and sports fashion brand there is. Nike has no direct competitors because there is no single brand which can compete directly with their range of sports and non-sports oriented gear, except for Reebok.
Nonprofit organization	An organization whose goals do not include making a personal profit for its owners is a nonprofit organization.
Enterprise	Enterprise refers to another name for a business organization. Other similar terms are business firm, sometimes simply business, sometimes simply firm, as well as company, and entity.
Expense	In accounting, an expense represents an event in which an asset is used up or a liability is incurred. In terms of the accounting equation, expenses reduce owners' equity.
Manufacturing	Production of goods primarily by the application of labor and capital to raw materials and other intermediate inputs, in contrast to agriculture, mining, forestry, fishing, and services a manufacturing.
Productivity	Productivity refers to the total output of goods and services in a given period of time divided by work hours.
Division of labor	Division of labor is generally speaking the specialization of cooperative labor in specific, circumscribed tasks and roles, intended to increase efficiency of output.
Labor	People's physical and mental talents and efforts that are used to help produce goods and services are called labor.
Job enlargement	A job enrichment strategy that involves combining a series of tasks into one challenging and interesting assignment is referred to as job enlargement.
Job enrichment	A motivational strategy that emphasizes motivating the worker through the job itself is called job enrichment.
Job rotation	A job enrichment strategy that involves moving employees from one job to another is a job rotation.
Conceptual skill	The ability to analyze and solve complex problems is called conceptual skill. Conceptual skill involves the formulation of ideas.
Trend	Trend refers to the long-term movement of an economic variable, such as its average rate of increase or decrease over enough years to encompass several business cycles.
Teamwork	That which occurs when group members work together in ways that utilize their skills well to

accomplish a purpose is called teamwork.

Core	A core is the set of feasible allocations in an economy that cannot be improved upon by subset of the set of the economy's consumers (a coalition). In construction, when the force in an element is within a certain center section, the core, the element will only be under compression.
Task identity	The degree to which employees perceive how their job impacts the overall production of a product or service is task identity.
Task significance	The measure of how much of a job has a substantial impact on the lives of other people, whether these people are in the immediate organization or in the world at large is task significance.
Inventory	Tangible property held for sale in the normal course of business or used in producing goods or services for sale is an inventory.
Performance appraisal	An evaluation in which the performance level of employees is measured against established standards to make decisions about promotions, compenzation, additional training, or firing is referred to as performance appraisal.
Strategic business unit	Strategic business unit is understood as a business unit within the overall corporate identity which is distinguishable from other business because it serves a defined external market where management can conduct strategic planning in relation to products and markets. When companies become really large, they are best thought of as being composed of a number of businesses
Business unit	The lowest level of the company which contains the set of functions that carry a product through its life span from concept through manufacture, distribution, sales and service is a business unit.
Portfolio	In finance, a portfolio is a collection of investments held by an institution or a private individual. Holding but not always a portfolio is part of an investment and risk-limiting strategy called diversification. By owning several assets, certain types of risk (in particular specific risk) can be reduced.
Management team	A management team is directly responsible for managing the day-to-day operations (and profitability) of a company.
Extension	Extension refers to an out-of-court settlement in which creditors agree to allow the firm more time to meet its financial obligations. A new repayment schedule will be developed, subject to the acceptance of creditors.
Contract	A contract is a "promise" or an "agreement" that is enforced or recognized by the law. In the civil law, a contract is considered to be part of the general law of obligations.
Sales forecast	Sales forecast refers to the maximum total sales of a product that a firm expects to sell during a specified time period under specified environmental conditions and its own marketing efforts.
Journal	Book of original entry, in which transactions are recorded in a general ledger system, is referred to as a journal.

Organizational culture	The mindset of employees, including their shared beliefs, values, and goals is called the organizational culture.
Core	A core is the set of feasible allocations in an economy that cannot be improved upon by subset of the set of the economy's consumers (a coalition). In construction, when the force in an element is within a certain center section, the core, the element will only be under compression.
Learning organization	A firm, which values continuous learning and is consistently looking to adapt and change with its environment is referred to as learning organization.
Innovation	Innovation refers to the first commercially successful introduction of a new product, the use of a new method of production, or the creation of a new form of business organization.
Process consultation	Process consultation involves interviewing people and observing work group processes to uncover interpersonal stumbling blocks and related problems. A change agent will then provide feedback aimed at improving the work process.
Team building	A term that describes the process of identifying roles for team members and helping the team members succeed in their roles is called team building.
Resistance to change	Resistance to change refers to an attitude or behavior that shows unwillingness to make or support a change.
Sponsorship	When the advertiser assumes responsibility for the production and usually the content of a television program as well as the advertising that appears within it, we have sponsorship.
Brand image	The advertising metric that measures the type and favorability of consumer perceptions of the brand is referred to as the brand image.
Interest	In finance and economics, interest is the price paid by a borrower for the use of a lender's money. In other words, interest is the amount of paid to "rent" money for a period of time.
Brand	A name, symbol, or design that identifies the goods or services of one seller or group of sellers and distinguishes them from the goods and services of competitors is a brand.
Marketing	Promoting and selling products or services to customers, or prospective customers, is referred to as marketing.
Driving force	The key external pressure that will shape the future for an organization is a driving force. The driving force in an industry are the main underlying causes of changing industry and competitive conditions.
Principal	In agency law, one under whose direction an agent acts and for whose benefit that agent acts is a principal.
Technology	The body of knowledge and techniques that can be used to combine economic resources to produce goods and services is called technology.
Budget	Budget refers to an account, usually for a year, of the planned expenditures and the expected receipts of an entity. For a government, the receipts are tax revenues.
Economic forces	Forces that affect the availability, production, and distribution of a society's resources among competing users are referred to as economic forces.
Management team	A management team is directly responsible for managing the day-to-day operations (and profitability) of a company.
Management	Management characterizes the process of leading and directing all or part of an organization, often a business, through the deployment and manipulation of resources. Early twentieth-century management writer Mary Parker Follett defined management as "the art of getting things done through people."

Margin	A deposit by a buyer in stocks with a seller or a stockbroker, as security to cover fluctuations in the market in reference to stocks that the buyer has purchased but for which he has not paid is a margin. Commodities are also traded on margin.
Social forces	The demographic characteristics of the population and its values in the environment are a social forces.
Strike	The withholding of labor services by an organized group of workers is referred to as a strike.
Demographic	A demographic is a term used in marketing and broadcasting, to describe a demographic grouping or a market segment.
Management functions	Management functions were set forth by Henri Fayol; they include planning, organizing, leading, and controling.
Evaluation	The consumer's appraisal of the product or brand on important attributes is called evaluation.
Variable	A variable is something measured by a number; it is used to analyze what happens to other things when the size of that number changes.
Market	A market is, as defined in economics, a social arrangement that allows buyers and sellers to discover information and carry out a voluntary exchange of goods or services.
Merger	Merger refers to the combination of two firms into a single firm.
Organizational structure	Organizational structure is the way in which the interrelated groups of an organization are constructed. From a managerial point of view the main concerns are ensuring effective communication and coordination.
Competitive advantage	A business is said to have a competitive advantage when its unique strengths, often based on cost, quality, time, and innovation, offer consumers a greater percieved value and there by differtiating it from its competitors.
Productivity	Productivity refers to the total output of goods and services in a given period of time divided by work hours.
Gain	In finance, gain is a profit or an increase in value of an investment such as a stock or bond. Gain is calculated by fair market value or the proceeds from the sale of the investment minus the sum of the purchase price and all costs associated with it.
Recovery	Characterized by rizing output, falling unemployment, rizing profits, and increasing economic activity following a decline is a recovery.
Inputs	The inputs used by a firm or an economy are the labor, raw materials, electricity and other resources it uses to produce its outputs.
Automation	Automation allows machines to do work previously accomplished by people.
Management information system	A computer-based system that provides information and support for effective managerial decision makin is referred to as a management information system.
Information system	An information system is a system whether automated or manual, that comprises people, machines, and/or methods organized to collect, process, transmit, and disseminate data that represent user information.
Aid	Assistance provided by countries and by international institutions such as the World Bank to developing countries in the form of monetary grants, loans at low interest rates, in kind, or a combination of these is called aid. Aid can also refer to assistance of any type rendered to benefit some group or individual.

Go to **Cram101.com** for the Practice Tests for this Chapter.

Production	The creation of finished goods and services using the factors of production: land, labor, capital, entrepreneurship, and knowledge.
Inventory	Tangible property held for sale in the normal course of business or used in producing goods or services for sale is an inventory.
Jury	A body of lay persons, selected by lot, or by some other fair and impartial means, to ascertain, under the guidance of the judge, the truth in questions of fact arising either in civil litigation or a criminal process is referred to as jury.
Structural change	Changes in the relative importance of different areas of an economy over time, usually measured in terms of their share of output, employment, or total spending is structural change.
Market niche	A market niche or niche market is a focused, targetable portion of a market. By definition, then, a business that focuses on a niche market is addressing a need for a product or service that is not being addressed by mainstream providers.
Bottom line	The bottom line is net income on the last line of a income statement.
Niche	In industry, a niche is a situation or an activity perfectly suited to a person. A niche can imply a working position or an area suited to a person who occupies it. Basically, a job where a person is able to succeed and thrive.
Effective manager	Leader of a team that consistently achieves high performance goals is an effective manager.
Assignment	A transfer of property or some right or interest is referred to as assignment.
Security	Security refers to a claim on the borrower future income that is sold by the borrower to the lender. A security is a type of transferable interest representing financial value.
Trust	An arrangement in which shareholders of independent firms agree to give up their stock in exchange for trust certificates that entitle them to a share of the trust's common profits.
Consideration	Consideration in contract law, a basic requirement for an enforceable agreement under traditional contract principles, defined in this text as legal value, bargained for and given in exchange for an act or promise. In corporation law, cash or property contributed to a corporation in exchange for shares, or a promise to contribute such cash or property.
Proactive	To be proactive is to act before a situation becomes a source of confrontation or crisis. It is the opposite of "retroactive," which refers to actions taken after an event.
Bond	Bond refers to a debt instrument, issued by a borrower and promising a specified stream of payments to the purchaser, usually regular interest payments plus a final repayment of principal.
Jargon	Jargon is terminology, much like slang, that relates to a specific activity, profession, or group. It develops as a kind of shorthand, to express ideas that are frequently discussed between members of a group, and can also have the effect of distinguishing those belonging to a group from those who are not.
Foundation	A Foundation is a type of philanthropic organization set up by either individuals or institutions as a legal entity (either as a corporation or trust) with the purpose of distributing grants to support causes in line with the goals of the foundation.
Mergers and acquisitions	The phrase mergers and acquisitions refers to the aspect of corporate finance strategy and management dealing with the merging and acquiring of different companies as well as other assets. Usually mergers occur in a friendly setting where executives from the respective companies participate in a due diligence process to ensure a successful combination of all parts.

Acquisition	A company's purchase of the property and obligations of another company is an acquisition.
Alignment	Term that refers to optimal coordination among disparate departments and divisions within a firm is referred to as alignment.
Product innovation	The development and sale of a new or improved product is a product innovation. Production of a new product on a commercial basis.
Process innovation	The development and use of new or improved production or distribution methods is called process innovation. It is an approach in business process reengineering by which radical changes are made through innovations.
Industry	A group of firms that produce identical or similar products is an industry. It is also used specifically to refer to an area of economic production focused on manufacturing which involves large amounts of capital investment before any profit can be realized, also called "heavy industry".
Competitor	Other organizations in the same industry or type of business that provide a good or service to the same set of customers is referred to as a competitor.
Flat organization	Flat organization refers to a organizational structure with few or no levels of intervening management between staff and managers. The idea is that well-trained workers will be more productive when they are more directly involved in the decision making process, rather than closely supervized by many layers of management.
Authority	Authority in agency law, refers to an agent's ability to affect his principal's legal relations with third parties. Also used to refer to an actor's legal power or ability to do something. In addition, sometimes used to refer to a statute, case, or other legal source that justifies a particular result.
Sociotechnical systems	Organizational systems that integrate people and technology into high-performance work settings are referred to as sociotechnical systems.
Policy	Similar to a script in that a policy can be a less than completely rational decision-making method. Involves the use of a pre-existing set of decision steps for any problem that presents itself.
Scope	Scope of a project is the sum total of all projects products and their requirements or features.
Process improvement	Process improvement is the activity of elevating the performance of a process, especially that of a business process with regard to its goal.
Customer value	Customer value refers to the unique combination of benefits received by targeted buyers that includes quality, price, convenience, on-time delivery, and both before-sale and after-sale service.
Openness	Openness refers to the extent to which an economy is open, often measured by the ratio of its trade to GDP.
Service	Service refers to a "non tangible product" that is not embodied in a physical good and that typically effects some change in another product, person, or institution. Contrasts with good.
Quota	A government-imposed restriction on quantity, or sometimes on total value, used to restrict the import of something to a specific quantity is called a quota.
Supervisor	A Supervisor is an employee of an organization with some of the powers and responsibilities of management, occupying a role between true manager and a regular employee. A Supervisor position is typically the first step towards being promoted into a management role.

Go to **Cram101.com** for the Practice Tests for this Chapter.

Deming	Deming is widely credited with improving production in the United States during World War II, although he is perhaps best known for his work in Japan. There, from 1950 onward he taught top management how to improve design (and thus service), product quality, testing and sales (the latter through global markets).
Points	Loan origination fees that may be deductible as interest by a buyer of property. A seller of property who pays points reduces the selling price by the amount of the points paid for the buyer.
Systems view	A management viewpoint that focuses on the interactions between the various components that combine to produce a product or service is called systems view. The systems view focuses management on the system as the cause of quality problems.
Leadership	Management merely consists of leadership applied to business situations; or in other words: management forms a sub-set of the broader process of leadership.
Equal employment opportunity	The government's attempt to ensure that all individuals have an equal opportunity for employment, regardless of race, color, religion, sex, age, disability, or national origin is equal employment opportunity.
Affirmative action	Policies and programs that establish procedures for increasing employment and promotion for women and minorities are called affirmative action.
Personnel	A collective term for all of the employees of an organization. Personnel is also commonly used to refer to the personnel management function or the organizational unit responsible for administering personnel programs.
Valuing diversity	Valuing diversity refers to putting an end to the assumption that everyone who is not a member of the dominant group must assimilate. The first step is to recognize that diversity exists in organizations so that we can begin to manage it.
Preference	The act of a debtor in paying or securing one or more of his creditors in a manner more favorable to them than to other creditors or to the exclusion of such other creditors is a preference. In the absence of statute, a preference is perfectly good, but to be legal it must be bona fide, and not a mere subterfuge of the debtor to secure a future benefit to himself or to prevent the application of his property to his debts.
Synergy	Corporate synergy occurs when corporations interact congruently. A corporate synergy refers to a financial benefit that a corporation expects to realize when it merges with or acquires another corporation.
Diversity training	Diversity training refers to training designed to change employee attitudes about diversity and/or develop skills needed to work with a diverse workforce.
Managing diversity	Building systems and a climate that unite different people in a common pursuit without undermining their individual strengths is managing diversity.
Assessment	Collecting information and providing feedback to employees about their behavior, communication style, or skills is an assessment.
Equity	Equity is the name given to the set of legal principles, in countries following the English common law tradition, which supplement strict rules of law where their application would operate harshly, so as to achieve what is sometimes referred to as "natural justice."
Equal Pay Act	Legislation passed in the Federal Government of the United States in 1963 that made it illegal to pay men and women different wage rates for equal work on jobs that require equal skill, effort, and responsibility and are performed under similar working conditions is the Equal Pay Act of 1963.
Glass ceiling	Glass ceiling refers to a term that refers to the many barriers that can exist to thwart a

woman's rise to the top of an organization; one that provides a view of the top, but a ceiling on how far a woman can go.

Sexual harassment	Unwelcome sexual advances, requests for sexual favors, and other conduct of a sexual nature is called sexual harassment.
Mentoring	Mentoring refers to a developmental relationship between a more experienced mentor and a less experienced partner referred to as a mentee or protégé. Usually - but not necessarily - the mentor/protégé pair will be of the same sex.
Mentor	An experienced employee who supervises, coaches, and guides lower-level employees by introducing them to the right people and generally being their organizational sponsor is a mentor.
Organizational development	The application of behavioral science knowledge in a longrange effort to improve an organization's ability to cope with change in its external environment and increase its problem-solving capabilities is referred to as organizational development.
Change agent	A change agent is someone who engages either deliberately or whose behavior results in social, cultural or behavioral change. This can be studied scientifically and effective techniques can be discovered and employed.
Consultant	A professional that provides expert advice in a particular field or area in which customers occassionaly require this type of knowledge is a consultant.
Agent	A person who makes economic decisions for another economic actor. A hired manager operates as an agent for a firm's owner.
Unfreezing	The process by which people become aware of the need for change is unfreezing.
Status quo	Status quo is a Latin term meaning the present, current, existing state of affairs.
Refreezing	The process of making new behaviors relatively permanent and resistant to further change is refreezing.
Comprehensive	A comprehensive refers to a layout accurate in size, color, scheme, and other necessary details to show how a final ad will look. For presentation only, never for reproduction.
Intervention	Intervention refers to an activity in which a government buys or sells its currency in the foreign exchange market in order to affect its currency's exchange rate.
Training and development	All attempts to improve productivity by increasing an employee's ability to perform is training and development.
Action plan	Action plan refers to a written document that includes the steps the trainee and manager will take to ensure that training transfers to the job.
Allocate	Allocate refers to the assignment of income for various tax purposes. A multistate corporation's nonbusiness income usually is distributed to the state where the nonbusiness assets are located; it is not apportioned with the rest of the entity's income.
Job enrichment	A motivational strategy that emphasizes motivating the worker through the job itself is called job enrichment.
Firm	An organization that employs resources to produce a good or service for profit and owns and operates one or more plants is referred to as a firm.
Internal environment	Variables that are under some degree of control by organizational members is the internal enviroment. Internal environment scans are conducted to identify an organization's internal capabilities, performance levels, strengths, and weaknesses.
Big Business	Big business is usually used as a pejorative reference to the significant economic and

	political power which large and powerful corporations (especially multinational corporations), are capable of wielding.
Fund	Independent accounting entity with a self-balancing set of accounts segregated for the purposes of carrying on specific activities is referred to as a fund.
Operation	A standardized method or technique that is performed repetitively, often on different materials resulting in different finished goods is called an operation.
Marketing strategy	Marketing strategy refers to the means by which a marketing goal is to be achieved, usually characterized by a specified target market and a marketing program to reach it.
License	A license in the sphere of Intellectual Property Rights (IPR) is a document, contract or agreement giving permission or the 'right' to a legally-definable entity to do something (such as manufacture a product or to use a service), or to apply something (such as a trademark), with the objective of achieving commercial gain.
Fiscal year	A fiscal year is a 12-month period used for calculating annual ("yearly") financial reports in businesses and other organizations. In many jurisdictions, regulatory laws regarding accounting require such reports once per twelve months, but do not require that the twelve months constitute a calendar year (i.e. January to December).
Revenue	Revenue is a U.S. business term for the amount of money that a company receives from its activities, mostly from sales of products and/or services to customers.
Profit	Profit refers to the return to the resource entrepreneurial ability; total revenue minus total cost.
Manufacturing	Production of goods primarily by the application of labor and capital to raw materials and other intermediate inputs, in contrast to agriculture, mining, forestry, fishing, and services a manufacturing.
Preparation	Preparation refers to usually the first stage in the creative process. It includes education and formal training.
Appreciation	Appreciation refers to a rise in the value of a country's currency on the exchange market, relative either to a particular other currency or to a weighted average of other currencies. The currency is said to appreciate. Opposite of 'depreciation.' Appreciation can also refer to the increase in value of any asset.

Training and development	All attempts to improve productivity by increasing an employee's ability to perform is training and development.
Performance appraisal	An evaluation in which the performance level of employees is measured against established standards to make decisions about promotions, compenzation, additional training, or firing is referred to as performance appraisal.
Evaluation	The consumer's appraisal of the product or brand on important attributes is called evaluation.
Labor relations	The field of labor relations looks at the relationship between management and workers, particularly groups of workers represented by a labor union.
Labor	People's physical and mental talents and efforts that are used to help produce goods and services are called labor.
Brief	Brief refers to a statement of a party's case or legal arguments, usually prepared by an attorney. Also used to make legal arguments before appellate courts.
Tort	In the common law, a tort is a civil wrong, other than a breach of contract, for which the law provides a remedy. A tort is a breach of a non-contractual duty potentially owed to the entire world, imposed by law. The majority of legal claims are brought in tort.
Collective bargaining	Collective bargaining refers to the negotiation of labor contracts between labor unions and firms or government entities.
Human resources	Human resources refers to the individuals within the firm, and to the portion of the firm's organization that deals with hiring, firing, training, and other personnel issues.
Management	Management characterizes the process of leading and directing all or part of an organization, often a business, through the deployment and manipulation of resources. Early twentieth-century management writer Mary Parker Follett defined management as "the art of getting things done through people."
Staffing	Staffing refers to a management function that includes hiring, motivating, and retaining the best people available to accomplish the company's objectives.
Job analysis	Job analysis refers to a study of what is done by employees who hold various job titles. It refers to various methodologies for analyzing the requirements of a job.
Service	Service refers to a "non tangible product" that is not embodied in a physical good and that typically effects some change in another product, person, or institution. Contrasts with good.
Competitor	Other organizations in the same industry or type of business that provide a good or service to the same set of customers is referred to as a competitor.
Civil rights act of 1964	The Civil Rights Act of 1964 is a federal law that, in Title VII, outlaws discrimination based on race, color, religion, gender, or national origin in hiring, promoting, and compensating workers.
Equal employment opportunity	The government's attempt to ensure that all individuals have an equal opportunity for employment, regardless of race, color, religion, sex, age, disability, or national origin is equal employment opportunity.
Class action	In law, a class action is an equitable procedural device used in litigation to determine the rights of and remedies, if any, for large numbers of people whose cases involve common questions of law and fact. Traditionally, they have been used to litigate antitrust and securities lawsuits, as well as school desegregation cases, but more recently have been used for a wide range of legal disputes that involve a large number of injured parties.

Bona fide occupational qualification	A job qualification based on race, sex, religion, and so on that an employer asserts is a necessary qualification for the job is a bona fide occupational qualification.
Operation	A standardized method or technique that is performed repetitively, often on different materials resulting in different finished goods is called an operation.
Applicant	In many tribunal and administrative law suits, the person who initiates the claim is called the applicant.
Affiliation	A relationship with other websites in which a company can cross-promote and is credited for sales that accrue through their site is an affiliation.
Preference	The act of a debtor in paying or securing one or more of his creditors in a manner more favorable to them than to other creditors or to the exclusion of such other creditors is a preference. In the absence of statute, a preference is perfectly good, but to be legal it must be bona fide, and not a mere subterfuge of the debtor to secure a future benefit to himself or to prevent the application of his property to his debts.
Garnishment	A statutory proceeding whereby money, property, wages, or credits of the defendant that are in the hands of a third party are seized to satisfy a judgment or legally valid claim that the plaintiff has against the defendant is called garnishment.
Credit	Credit refers to a recording as positive in the balance of payments, any transaction that gives rise to a payment into the country, such as an export, the sale of an asset, or borrowing from abroad.
Draft	A signed, written order by which one party instructs another party to pay a specified sum to a third party, at sight or at a specific date is a draft.
Trade association	An industry trade group or trade association is generally a public relations organization founded and funded by corporations that operate in a specific industry. Its purpose is generally to promote that industry through PR activities such as advertizing, education, political donations, political pressure, publishing, and astroturfing.
Union	A worker association that bargains with employers over wages and working conditions is called a union.
Termination	The ending of a corporation that occurs only after the winding-up of the corporation's affairs, the liquidation of its assets, and the distribution of the proceeds to the claimants are referred to as a termination.
Retrenchment	Retrenchment means the reduction of expenditures in order to become financially stable. It is a tactical concept similar to downsizing.
Layoff	A layoff is the termination of an employee or (more commonly) a group of employees for business reasons, such as the decision that certain positions are no longer necessary.
Sales forecast	Sales forecast refers to the maximum total sales of a product that a firm expects to sell during a specified time period under specified environmental conditions and its own marketing efforts.
Negotiation	Negotiation is the process whereby interested parties resolve disputes, agree upon courses of action, bargain for individual or collective advantage, and/or attempt to craft outcomes which serve their mutual interests.
Contract	A contract is a "promise" or an "agreement" that is enforced or recognized by the law. In the civil law, a contract is considered to be part of the general law of obligations.
Strategic human resource	Strategic human resource management refers to a pattern of planned human resource deployments and activities intended to enable an organization to achieve its goals.

management	
Human resource management	The process of evaluating human resource needs, finding people to fill those needs, and getting the best work from each employee by providing the right incentives and job environment, all with the goal of meeting the needs of the firm are called human resource management.
Resource management	Resource management is the efficient and effective deployment of an organization's resources when they are needed. Such resources may include financial resources, inventory, human skills, production resources, or information technology.
General manager	A manager who is responsible for several departments that perform different functions is called general manager.
Consultant	A professional that provides expert advice in a particular field or area in which customers occassionaly require this type of knowledge is a consultant.
Trend	Trend refers to the long-term movement of an economic variable, such as its average rate of increase or decrease over enough years to encompass several business cycles.
Compliance	A type of influence process where a receiver accepts the position advocated by a source to obtain favorable outcomes or to avoid punishment is the compliance.
Administration	Administration refers to the management and direction of the affairs of governments and institutions; a collective term for all policymaking officials of a government; the execution and implementation of public policy.
Strategic plan	The formal document that presents the ways and means by which a strategic goal will be achieved is a strategic plan. A long-term flexible plan that does not regulate activities but rather outlines the means to achieve certain results, and provides the means to alter the course of action should the desired ends change.
Policy	Similar to a script in that a policy can be a less than completely rational decision-making method. Involves the use of a pre-existing set of decision steps for any problem that presents itself.
Regulation	Regulation refers to restrictions state and federal laws place on business with regard to the conduct of its activities.
Equity	Equity is the name given to the set of legal principles, in countries following the English common law tradition, which supplement strict rules of law where their application would operate harshly, so as to achieve what is sometimes referred to as "natural justice."
Collaboration	Collaboration occurs when the interaction between groups is very important to goal attainment and the goals are compatible. Wherein people work together —applying both to the work of individuals as well as larger collectives and societies.
Marketing	Promoting and selling products or services to customers, or prospective customers, is referred to as marketing.
Public relations	Public relations refers to the management function that evaluates public attitudes, changes policies and procedures in response to the public's requests, and executes a program of action and information to earn public understanding and acceptance.
Promotion	Promotion refers to all the techniques sellers use to motivate people to buy products or services. An attempt by marketers to inform people about products and to persuade them to participate in an exchange.
Fund	Independent accounting entity with a self-balancing set of accounts segregated for the purposes of carrying on specific activities is referred to as a fund.

Go to **Cram101.com** for the Practice Tests for this Chapter.

Personnel	A collective term for all of the employees of an organization. Personnel is also commonly used to refer to the personnel management function or the organizational unit responsible for administering personnel programs.
Proactive	To be proactive is to act before a situation becomes a source of confrontation or crisis. It is the opposite of "retroactive," which refers to actions taken after an event.
Leadership	Management merely consists of leadership applied to business situations; or in other words: management forms a sub-set of the broader process of leadership.
Reasonable accommodation	Making facilities readily accessible to and usable by individuals with physical or mental limitations is referred to as reasonable accommodation.
Accommodation	Accommodation is a term used to describe a delivery of nonconforming goods meant as a partial performance of a contract for the sale of goods, where a full performance is not possible.
Realistic job preview	Realistic job preview provides accurate information about the attractive and unattractive aspects of a job, working conditions, company, and location to ensure that potential employees develop appropriate expectations.
Recruitment	Recruitment refers to the set of activities used to obtain a sufficient number of the right people at the right time; its purpose is to select those who best meet the needs of the organization.
Advertising	Advertising refers to paid, nonpersonal communication through various media by organizations and individuals who are in some way identified in the advertising message.
Open position	An obligation to take or make delivery of an asset or currency in the future without cover, that is, without a matching obligation in the other direction that protects them from effects of change in the price of the asset or currency is an open position.
Bid	A bid price is a price offered by a buyer when he/she buys a good. In the context of stock trading on a stock exchange, the bid price is the highest price a buyer of a stock is willing to pay for a share of that given stock.
Career planning	Process in which individuals evaluate their abilities and interests, consider alternative career opportunities, establish career goals, and plan practical development activities is referred to as career planning.
Aid	Assistance provided by countries and by international institutions such as the World Bank to developing countries in the form of monetary grants, loans at low interest rates, in kind, or a combination of these is called aid. Aid can also refer to assistance of any type rendered to benefit some group or individual.
Supervisor	A Supervisor is an employee of an organization with some of the powers and responsibilities of management, occupying a role between true manager and a regular employee. A Supervisor position is typically the first step towards being promoted into a management role.
Technology	The body of knowledge and techniques that can be used to combine economic resources to produce goods and services is called technology.
Gap	In December of 1995, Gap became the first major North American retailer to accept independent monitoring of the working conditions in a contract factory producing its garments. Gap is the largest specialty retailer in the United States.
Screening	Screening in economics refers to a strategy of combating adverse selection, one of the potential decision-making complications in cases of asymmetric information.
Specialist	A specialist is a trader who makes a market in one or several stocks and holds the limit order book for those stocks.

Aptitude	An aptitude is an innate inborn ability to do a certain kind of work. Aptitudes may be physical or mental. Many of them have been identified and are testable.
Interest	In finance and economics, interest is the price paid by a borrower for the use of a lender's money. In other words, interest is the amount of paid to "rent" money for a period of time.
Assessment center	Assessment center refers to a process in which multiple raters evaluate employees' performance on a number of exercises.
Assessment	Collecting information and providing feedback to employees about their behavior, communication style, or skills is an assessment.
Interpersonal skills	Interpersonal skills are used to communicate with, understand, and motivate individuals and groups.
Trust	An arrangement in which shareholders of independent firms agree to give up their stock in exchange for trust certificates that entitle them to a share of the trust's common profits.
Turnover	Turnover in a financial context refers to the rate at which a provider of goods cycles through its average inventory. Turnover in a human resources context refers to the characteristic of a given company or industry, relative to rate at which an employer gains and loses staff.
Standing plan	An ongoing plan used to provide guidance for tasks performed repeatedly within the organization is a standing plan.
Standing	Standing refers to the legal requirement that anyone seeking to challenge a particular action in court must demonstrate that such action substantially affects his legitimate interests before he will be entitled to bring suit.
Complexity	The technical sophistication of the product and hence the amount of understanding required to use it is referred to as complexity. It is the opposite of simplicity.
Investment	Investment refers to spending for the production and accumulation of capital and additions to inventories. In a financial sense, buying an asset with the expectation of making a return.
Economy	The income, expenditures, and resources that affect the cost of running a business and household are called an economy.
Vestibule training	Training done in schools where employees are taught on equipment similar to that used on the job is referred to as vestibule training.
Needs assessment	The process used to determine if training is necessary is called needs assessment.
Training outcomes	A way to evaluate the effectiveness of a training program based on cognitive, skill-based, affective, and results outcomes are referred to as training outcomes.
Conceptual skill	The ability to analyze and solve complex problems is called conceptual skill. Conceptual skill involves the formulation of ideas.
Assignment	A transfer of property or some right or interest is referred to as assignment.
Complaint	The pleading in a civil case in which the plaintiff states his claim and requests relief is called complaint. In the common law, it is a formal legal document that sets out the basic facts and legal reasons that the filing party (the plaintiffs) believes are sufficient to support a claim against another person, persons, entity or entities (the defendants) that entitles the plaintiff(s) to a remedy (either money damages or injunctive relief).
Holding	The holding is a court's determination of a matter of law based on the issue presented in the particular case. In other words: under this law, with these facts, this result.
Industry	A group of firms that produce identical or similar products is an industry. It is also used

specifically to refer to an area of economic production focused on manufacturing which involves large amounts of capital investment before any profit can be realized, also called "heavy industry".

Feedback loop	Feedback loop consists of a response and feedback. It is a system where outputs are fed back into the system as inputs, increasing or decreasing effects.
Preparation	Preparation refers to usually the first stage in the creative process. It includes education and formal training.
Behaviorally Anchored Rating Scale	A performance appraisal approach that describes observable job behaviors, each of which is evaluated to determine good versus bad performance is referred to as behaviorally anchored rating scale.
Distribution	Distribution in economics, the manner in which total output and income is distributed among individuals or factors.
Management by objectives	Management by objectives is a process of agreeing upon objectives within an organization so that management and employees buy in to the objectives and understand what they are.
Middle management	Middle management refers to the level of management that includes general managers, division managers, and branch and plant managers who are responsible for tactical planning and controlling.
Market	A market is, as defined in economics, a social arrangement that allows buyers and sellers to discover information and carry out a voluntary exchange of goods or services.
Productivity	Productivity refers to the total output of goods and services in a given period of time divided by work hours.
Contribution	In business organization law, the cash or property contributed to a business by its owners is referred to as contribution.
Total cost	The sum of fixed cost and variable cost is referred to as total cost.
Firm	An organization that employs resources to produce a good or service for profit and owns and operates one or more plants is referred to as a firm.
Wage	The payment for the service of a unit of labor, per unit time. In trade theory, it is the only payment to labor, usually unskilled labor. In empirical work, wage data may exclude other compenzation, which must be added to get the total cost of employment.
Pay for Performance	A one-time cash payment to an investment center manager as a reward for meeting a predetermined criterion on a specified performance measure is referred to as pay for performance.
Incentive	An incentive is any factor (financial or non-financial) that provides a motive for a particular course of action, or counts as a reason for preferring one choice to the alternatives.
Production	The creation of finished goods and services using the factors of production: land, labor, capital, entrepreneurship, and knowledge.
Piece rate	Piece rate is a form of compenzation or payment in which a person is paid a given rate per item made.
Profit sharing	A compenzation plan in which payments are based on a measure of organization performance and do not become part of the employees' base salary is profit sharing.
Profit	Profit refers to the return to the resource entrepreneurial ability; total revenue minus total cost.

Go to **Cram101.com** for the Practice Tests for this Chapter.

Comparable worth	The concept that people in jobs that require similar levels of education, training, or skills should receive equal pay is called comparable worth.
Compensation package	The total array of money, incentives, benefits, perquisites, and awards provided by the organization to an employee is the compensation package.
Social Security	Social security primarily refers to a field of social welfare concerned with social protection, or protection against socially recognized conditions, including poverty, old age, disability, unemployment, families with children and others.
Security	Security refers to a claim on the borrower future income that is sold by the borrower to the lender. A security is a type of transferable interest representing financial value.
Health insurance	Health insurance is a type of insurance whereby the insurer pays the medical costs of the insured if the insured becomes sick due to covered causes, or due to accidents. The insurer may be a private organization or a government agency.
Insurance	Insurance refers to a system by which individuals can reduce their exposure to risk of large losses by spreading the risks among a large number of persons.
Pension	A pension is a steady income given to a person (usually after retirement). Pensions are typically payments made in the form of a guaranteed annuity to a retired or disabled employee.
Occupational Safety and Health Act	The Occupational Safety and Health Act is a United States federal law signed into law by President Richard M. Nixon on December 29, 1970. Its main aim was to ensure that employers provide their workers with an environment free from dangers to their safety and health.
National Labor Relations Board	The National Labor Relations Board is an independent agency of the United States Government charged with conducting elections for labor union representation and with investigating and remedying unfair labor practices.
National Labor Relations Act	The National Labor Relations Act is a 1935 United States federal law that protects the rights of most workers in the private sector to organize labor unions, to engage in collective bargaining, and to take part in strikes and other forms of concerted activity in support of their demands.
Unfair labor practice	Unfair labor practice refers to certain actions taken by employers that violate the National Labor Relations Act (NLRA) and other legislation.
Wagner Act	Wagner Act refers to guarantees the rights of workers to organize and bargain collectively and forbids employers from engaging in specified unfair labor practices. Also called National Labor Relations Act.
Injunction	Injunction refers to a court order directing a person or organization not to perform a certain act because the act would do irreparable damage to some other person or persons; a restraining order.
Decertification	The process by which workers take away a union's right to represent them is referred to as decertification.
Inflation	An increase in the overall price level of an economy, usually as measured by the CPI or by the implicit price deflator is called inflation.
Antitrust	Government intervention to alter market structure or prevent abuse of market power is called antitrust.
Exempt	Employees who are not covered by the Fair Labor Standards Act are exempt. Exempt employees are not eligible for overtime pay.
Executive branch	The executive branch is the part of government charged with implementing or enforcing the

laws. Consists of the President and Vice President.

Agent	A person who makes economic decisions for another economic actor. A hired manager operates as an agent for a firm's owner.
Option	A contract that gives the purchaser the option to buy or sell the underlying financial instrument at a specified price, called the exercise price or strike price, within a specific period of time.
Antitrust laws	Legislation that prohibits anticompetitive business activities such as price fixing, bid rigging, monopolization, and tying contracts is referred to as antitrust laws.
Collusion	Collusion refers to cooperation among firms to raise price and otherwise increase their profits.
Strike	The withholding of labor services by an organized group of workers is referred to as a strike.
Mediation	Mediation consists of a process of alternative dispute resolution in which a (generally) neutral third party using appropriate techniques, assists two or more parties to help them negotiate an agreement, with concrete effects, on a matter of common interest.
Compromise	Compromise occurs when the interaction is moderately important to meeting goals and the goals are neither completely compatible nor completely incompatible.
Lockout	Lockout refers to an action by a firm that forbids workers to return to work until a new collective bargaining contract is signed; a means of imposing costs on union workers in a collective bargaining dispute.
Grievance	A charge by employees that management is not abiding by the terms of the negotiated labormanagement agreement is the grievance.
Arbitration	Arbitration is a form of mediation or conciliation, where the mediating party is given power by the disputant parties to settle the dispute by making a finding. In practice arbitration is generally used as a substitute for judicial systems, particularly when the judicial processes are viewed as too slow, expensive or biased. Arbitration is also used by communities which lack formal law, as a substitute for formal law.
Outplacement	The process of placing employees in other positions or training once they have been separated from a job is outplacement. It helps people regain employment elsewhere.
Attrition	The practice of not hiring new employees to replace older employees who either quit or retire is referred to as attrition.
Exit interview	An interview conducted with departing employees to determine the reasons for their termination is called exit interview.
Mergers and acquisitions	The phrase mergers and acquisitions refers to the aspect of corporate finance strategy and management dealing with the merging and acquiring of different companies as well as other assets. Usually mergers occur in a friendly setting where executives from the respective companies participate in a due diligence process to ensure a successful combination of all parts.
Acquisition	A company's purchase of the property and obligations of another company is an acquisition.
Inventory	Tangible property held for sale in the normal course of business or used in producing goods or services for sale is an inventory.
Downturn	A decline in a stock market or economic cycle is a downturn.
Merger	Merger refers to the combination of two firms into a single firm.

Go to Cram101.com for the Practice Tests for this Chapter.

Nike	Because Nike creates goods for a wide range of sports, they have competition from every sports and sports fashion brand there is. Nike has no direct competitors because there is no single brand which can compete directly with their range of sports and non-sports oriented gear, except for Reebok.
Goodwill	Goodwill is an important accounting concept that describes the value of a business entity not directly attributable to its tangible assets and liabilities.
Margin	A deposit by a buyer in stocks with a seller or a stockbroker, as security to cover fluctuations in the market in reference to stocks that the buyer has purchased but for which he has not paid is a margin. Commodities are also traded on margin.
Allegation	An allegation is a statement of a fact by a party in a pleading, which the party claims it will prove. Allegations remain assertions without proof, only claims until they are proved.
Brand	A name, symbol, or design that identifies the goods or services of one seller or group of sellers and distinguishes them from the goods and services of competitors is a brand.
Budget	Budget refers to an account, usually for a year, of the planned expenditures and the expected receipts of an entity. For a government, the receipts are tax revenues.

Job satisfaction	Job satisfaction describes how content an individual is with his or her job. It is a relatively recent term since in previous centuries the jobs available to a particular person were often predetermined by the occupation of that person's parent.
Referent power	Referent power is individual power based on a high level of identification with, admiration of, or respect for the powerholder.
Reciprocity	An industrial buying practice in which two organizations agree to purchase each other's products and services is called reciprocity.
Coalition	An informal alliance among managers who support a specific goal is called coalition.
Tort	In the common law, a tort is a civil wrong, other than a breach of contract, for which the law provides a remedy. A tort is a breach of a non-contractual duty potentially owed to the entire world, imposed by law. The majority of legal claims are brought in tort.
Management	Management characterizes the process of leading and directing all or part of an organization, often a business, through the deployment and manipulation of resources. Early twentieth-century management writer Mary Parker Follett defined management as "the art of getting things done through people."
Negotiation	Negotiation is the process whereby interested parties resolve disputes, agree upon courses of action, bargain for individual or collective advantage, and/or attempt to craft outcomes which serve their mutual interests.
Organizational Behavior	The study of human behavior in organizational settings, the interface between human behavior and the organization, and the organization itself is called organizational behavior.
Organizational development	The application of behavioral science knowledge in a longrange effort to improve an organization's ability to cope with change in its external environment and increase its problem-solving capabilities is referred to as organizational development.
Fragmentation	Fragmentation refers to the splitting of production processes into separate parts that can be done in different locations, including in different countries.
Loyalty	Marketers tend to define customer loyalty as making repeat purchases. Some argue that it should be defined attitudinally as a strongly positive feeling about the brand.
Channel	Channel, in communications (sometimes called communications channel), refers to the medium used to convey information from a sender (or transmitter) to a receiver.
Big five personality traits	A set of fundamental traits that are especially relevant to organizations are the big five personality traits.
Machiavellianism	Machiavellianism refers to a personality trait. People who possess this trait behave to gain power and to control the behavior of others.
Market research	Market research is the process of systematic gathering, recording and analyzing of data about customers, competitors and the market. Market research can help create a business plan, launch a new product or service, fine tune existing products and services, expand into new markets etc. It can be used to determine which portion of the population will purchase the product/service, based on variables like age, gender, location and income level. It can be found out what market characteristics your target market has.
Market	A market is, as defined in economics, a social arrangement that allows buyers and sellers to discover information and carry out a voluntary exchange of goods or services.
Closing	The finalization of a real estate sales transaction that passes title to the property from the seller to the buyer is referred to as a closing. Closing is a sales term which refers to the process of making a sale. It refers to reaching the final step, which may be an exchange

of money or acquiring a signature.

Television network	Television network refers to the provider of news and programming to a series of affiliated local television stations.
Competitor	Other organizations in the same industry or type of business that provide a good or service to the same set of customers is referred to as a competitor.
Conscientiou-ness	Conscientiousness is the trait of being painstaking and careful, or the quality of being in accord with the dictates of one's conscience.Conscientiousness includes traits such as self-discipline, carefulness, thoroughness, orderedness, deliberation (the tendency to think carefully before acting) and need for achievement.
Openness	Openness refers to the extent to which an economy is open, often measured by the ratio of its trade to GDP.
Assessment	Collecting information and providing feedback to employees about their behavior, communication style, or skills is an assessment.
Attribution	Under certain circumstances, the tax law applies attribution rules to assign to one taxpayer the ownership interest of another taxpayer.
Contract	A contract is a "promise" or an "agreement" that is enforced or recognized by the law. In the civil law, a contract is considered to be part of the general law of obligations.
Union	A worker association that bargains with employers over wages and working conditions is called a union.
Bankruptcy	Bankruptcy is a legally declared inability or impairment of ability of an individual or organization to pay their creditors.
Evaluation	The consumer's appraisal of the product or brand on important attributes is called evaluation.
Diversity training	Diversity training refers to training designed to change employee attitudes about diversity and/or develop skills needed to work with a diverse workforce.
Pygmalion effect	The Pygmalion effect or Rosenthal effect refers to situations in which individuals perform better than others simply because they are expected to do so.
Workplace behavior	The pattern of action by the members of an organization that directly or indirectly influences organizational effectiveness is workplace behavior.
Preference	The act of a debtor in paying or securing one or more of his creditors in a manner more favorable to them than to other creditors or to the exclusion of such other creditors is a preference. In the absence of statute, a preference is perfectly good, but to be legal it must be bona fide, and not a mere subterfuge of the debtor to secure a future benefit to himself or to prevent the application of his property to his debts.
Teamwork	That which occurs when group members work together in ways that utilize their skills well to accomplish a purpose is called teamwork.
Turnover	Turnover in a financial context refers to the rate at which a provider of goods cycles through its average inventory. Turnover in a human resources context refers to the characteristic of a given company or industry, relative to rate at which an employer gains and loses staff.
Gain	In finance, gain is a profit or an increase in value of an investment such as a stock or bond. Gain is calculated by fair market value or the proceeds from the sale of the investment minus the sum of the purchase price and all costs associated with it.
Brand	A name, symbol, or design that identifies the goods or services of one seller or group of

	sellers and distinguishes them from the goods and services of competitors is a brand.
Nike	Because Nike creates goods for a wide range of sports, they have competition from every sports and sports fashion brand there is. Nike has no direct competitors because there is no single brand which can compete directly with their range of sports and non-sports oriented gear, except for Reebok.
Coercive power	Coercive power refers to the extent to which a person has the ability to punish or physically or psychologically harm someone else.
Position power	Position power refers to power manager's hold due to their role in the organization. May include a manager's network of contacts, legitimate authority and control over information, rewards, punishments, and the work environment.
Compliance	A type of influence process where a receiver accepts the position advocated by a source to obtain favorable outcomes or to avoid punishment is the compliance.
Coercion	Economic coercion is when an agent puts economic pressure onto the victim. The most common example of this is cutting off the supply to an essential resource, such as water.
Wage	The payment for the service of a unit of labor, per unit time. In trade theory, it is the only payment to labor, usually unskilled labor. In empirical work, wage data may exclude other compenzation, which must be added to get the total cost of employment.
Trust	An arrangement in which shareholders of independent firms agree to give up their stock in exchange for trust certificates that entitle them to a share of the trust's common profits.
Legitimate power	Legitimate power refers to power that is granted by virtue of one's position in the organization.
Authority	Authority in agency law, refers to an agent's ability to affect his principal's legal relations with third parties. Also used to refer to an actor's legal power or ability to do something. In addition, sometimes used to refer to a statute, case, or other legal source that justifies a particular result.
Charisma	A form of interpersonal attraction that inspires support and acceptance from others is charisma. It refers especially to a quality in certain people who easily draw the attention and admiration (or even hatred if the charisma is negative) of others due to a "magnetic" quality of personality and/or appearance.
Expert power	The extent to which a person controls information that is valuable to someone else is referred to as expert power.
Monopoly	A monopoly is defined as a persistent market situation where there is only one provider of a kind of product or service.
Needs theory	Henry Murray (1893-1988), developed a personality theory during the 1930s up to the 1960s, which he called the Needs Theory. A need in this theory is defined as 'the potentiality or readiness to respond in a certain way under given circumstances'.
Credibility	The extent to which a source is perceived as having knowledge, skill, or experience relevant to a communication topic and can be trusted to give an unbiased opinion or present objective information on the issue is called credibility.
Leadership	Management merely consists of leadership applied to business situations; or in other words: management forms a sub-set of the broader process of leadership.
Interest	In finance and economics, interest is the price paid by a borrower for the use of a lender's money. In other words, interest is the amount of paid to "rent" money for a period of time.
Committee	A long-lasting, sometimes permanent team in the organization structure created to deal with

tasks that recur regularly is the committee.

Promotion	Promotion refers to all the techniques sellers use to motivate people to buy products or services. An attempt by marketers to inform people about products and to persuade them to participate in an exchange.
Argument	The discussion by counsel for the respective parties of their contentions on the law and the facts of the case being tried in order to aid the jury in arriving at a correct and just conclusion is called argument.
Capitalism	Capitalism refers to an economic system in which capital is mostly owned by private individuals and corporations. Contrasts with communism.
In kind	Referring to a payment made with goods instead of money is an in kind. An expression relating to the insurer's right in many Property contracts to replace damaged objects with new or equivalent (in kind) material, rather than to pay a cash benefit.
Compromise	Compromise occurs when the interaction is moderately important to meeting goals and the goals are neither completely compatible nor completely incompatible.
Forming	The first stage of team development, where the team is formed and the objectives for the team are set is referred to as forming.
Trade secret	Trade secret refers to a secret formula, pattern, process, program, device, method, technique, or compilation of information that is used in its owner's business and affords that owner a competitive advantage. Trade secrets are protected by state law.
Dysfunctional conflict	Conflict that is responsible for hindering group performance is dysfunctional conflict.
Commercialism	Commercialism, in its original meaning, is the practices, methods, aims, and spirit of commerce or business. Today, however, it is mainly used as a critical term, referring to the tendency within capitalism to try to turn everything in life into objects and services that are sold for the purpose of generating profit; commercialization, where the value of everything, including such intangible things as happiness, health and beauty become measured in purely commercial, materialistic terms, and where public services are being privatized or outsourced to private companies.
Sponsorship	When the advertiser assumes responsibility for the production and usually the content of a television program as well as the advertising that appears within it, we have sponsorship.
Revenue	Revenue is a U.S. business term for the amount of money that a company receives from its activities, mostly from sales of products and/or services to customers.
Innovation	Innovation refers to the first commercially successful introduction of a new product, the use of a new method of production, or the creation of a new form of business organization.
Conflict management	Conflict management refers to the long-term management of intractable conflicts. It is the label for the variety of ways by which people handle grievances -- standing up for what they consider to be right and against what they consider to be wrong.
Accommodation	Accommodation is a term used to describe a delivery of nonconforming goods meant as a partial performance of a contract for the sale of goods, where a full performance is not possible.
Consideration	Consideration in contract law, a basic requirement for an enforceable agreement under traditional contract principles, defined in this text as legal value, bargained for and given in exchange for an act or promise. In corporation law, cash or property contributed to a corporation in exchange for shares, or a promise to contribute such cash or property.
Expense	In accounting, an expense represents an event in which an asset is used up or a liability is incurred. In terms of the accounting equation, expenses reduce owners' equity.

Go to **Cram101.com** for the Practice Tests for this Chapter.

Conflict resolution	Conflict resolution is the process of resolving a dispute or a conflict. Successful conflict resolution occurs by providing each side's needs, and adequately addressing their interests so that they are each satisfied with the outcome. Conflict resolution aims to end conflicts before they start or lead to physical fighting.
Cooperative	A business owned and controlled by the people who use it, producers, consumers, or workers with similar needs who pool their resources for mutual gain is called cooperative.
Collaboration	Collaboration occurs when the interaction between groups is very important to goal attainment and the goals are compatible. Wherein people work together —applying both to the work of individuals as well as larger collectives and societies.
Allocate	Allocate refers to the assignment of income for various tax purposes. A multistate corporation's nonbusiness income usually is distributed to the state where the nonbusiness assets are located; it is not apportioned with the rest of the entity's income.
Fund	Independent accounting entity with a self-balancing set of accounts segregated for the purposes of carrying on specific activities is referred to as a fund.
Task force	A temporary team or committee formed to solve a specific short-term problem involving several departments is the task force.
Service	Service refers to a "non tangible product" that is not embodied in a physical good and that typically effects some change in another product, person, or institution. Contrasts with good.
Budget	Budget refers to an account, usually for a year, of the planned expenditures and the expected receipts of an entity. For a government, the receipts are tax revenues.
Labor	People's physical and mental talents and efforts that are used to help produce goods and services are called labor.
Effective manager	Leader of a team that consistently achieves high performance goals is an effective manager.
Collective bargaining	Collective bargaining refers to the negotiation of labor contracts between labor unions and firms or government entities.
Fixed price	Fixed price is a phrase used to mean that no bargaining is allowed over the price of a good or, less commonly, a service.
Context	The effect of the background under which a message often takes on more and richer meaning is a context. Context is especially important in cross-cultural interactions because some cultures are said to be high context or low context.
Tradeoff	The sacrifice of some or all of one economic goal, good, or service to achieve some other goal, good, or service is a tradeoff.
Option	A contract that gives the purchaser the option to buy or sell the underlying financial instrument at a specified price, called the exercise price or strike price, within a specific period of time.
Objection	In the trial of a case the formal remonstrance made by counsel to something that has been said or done, in order to obtain the court's ruling thereon is an objection.
Agent	A person who makes economic decisions for another economic actor. A hired manager operates as an agent for a firm's owner.
Profit	Profit refers to the return to the resource entrepreneurial ability; total revenue minus total cost.
Complexity	The technical sophistication of the product and hence the amount of understanding required to

use it is referred to as complexity. It is the opposite of simplicity.

Concession	A concession is a business operated under a contract or license associated with a degree of exclusivity in exploiting a business within a certain geographical area. For example, sports arenas or public parks may have concession stands; and public services such as water supply may be operated as concessions.
Mistake	In contract law a mistake is incorrect understanding by one or more parties to a contract and may be used as grounds to invalidate the agreement. Common law has identified three different types of mistake in contract: unilateral mistake, mutual mistake, and common mistake.
Respondent	Respondent refers to a term often used to describe the party charged in an administrative proceeding. The party adverse to the appellant in a case appealed to a higher court.
Complaint	The pleading in a civil case in which the plaintiff states his claim and requests relief is called complaint. In the common law, it is a formal legal document that sets out the basic facts and legal reasons that the filing party (the plaintiffs) believes are sufficient to support a claim against another person, persons, entity or entities (the defendants) that entitles the plaintiff(s) to a remedy (either money damages or injunctive relief).
Appeal	Appeal refers to the act of asking an appellate court to overturn a decision after the trial court's final judgment has been entered.
Arbitration	Arbitration is a form of mediation or conciliation, where the mediating party is given power by the disputant parties to settle the dispute by making a finding. In practice arbitration is generally used as a substitute for judicial systems, particularly when the judicial processes are viewed as too slow, expensive or biased. Arbitration is also used by communities which lack formal law, as a substitute for formal law.
Mediation	Mediation consists of a process of alternative dispute resolution in which a (generally) neutral third party using appropriate techniques, assists two or more parties to help them negotiate an agreement, with concrete effects, on a matter of common interest.
Stress management	An active approach to deal with stress that is influencing behavior is stress management.
Productivity	Productivity refers to the total output of goods and services in a given period of time divided by work hours.
Organizational culture	The mindset of employees, including their shared beliefs, values, and goals is called the organizational culture.
Participative management	Participative management or participatory management is the practice of empowering employees to participate in organizational decision making.
Production	The creation of finished goods and services using the factors of production: land, labor, capital, entrepreneurship, and knowledge.
Time management	Time Management refers to tools or techniques for planning and scheduling time, usually with the aim to increase the effectiveness and/or efficiency of personal and corporate time use.
Balance	In banking and accountancy, the outstanding balance is the amount of money owned, (or due), that remains in a deposit account (or a loan account) at a given date, after all past remittances, payments and withdrawal have been accounted for. It can be positive (then, in the balance sheet of a firm, it is an asset) or negative (a liability).
Support network	A group of two or more trainees who agree to meet and discuss their progress in using learned capabilities on the job is referred to as support network.
Analogy	Analogy is either the cognitive process of transferring information from a particular subject to another particular subject (the target), or a linguistic expression corresponding to such

a process. In a narrower sense, analogy is an inference or an argument from a particular to another particular, as opposed to deduction, induction, and abduction, where at least one of the premises or the conclusion is general.

Direct relationship	Direct relationship refers to the relationship between two variables that change in the same direction, for example, product price and quantity supplied.
Chain of command	An unbroken line of authority that links all individuals in the organization and specifies who reports to whom is a chain of command. The concept of chain of command also implies that higher rank alone does not entitle a person to give commands.
Margin	A deposit by a buyer in stocks with a seller or a stockbroker, as security to cover fluctuations in the market in reference to stocks that the buyer has purchased but for which he has not paid is a margin. Commodities are also traded on margin.
Big Business	Big business is usually used as a pejorative reference to the significant economic and political power which large and powerful corporations (especially multinational corporations), are capable of wielding.
Punitive	Damages designed to punish flagrant wrongdoers and to deter them and others from engaging in similar conduct in the future are called punitive.
Charter	Charter refers to an instrument or authority from the sovereign power bestowing the right or power to do business under the corporate form of organization. Also, the organic law of a city or town, and representing a portion of the statute law of the state.
Organizational politics	Organizational politics occurs when power sources and influence tactics are used to serve personal goals or motives.
General manager	A manager who is responsible for several departments that perform different functions is called general manager.
Preparation	Preparation refers to usually the first stage in the creative process. It includes education and formal training.

Leadership	Management merely consists of leadership applied to business situations; or in other words: management forms a sub-set of the broader process of leadership.
Management	Management characterizes the process of leading and directing all or part of an organization, often a business, through the deployment and manipulation of resources. Early twentieth-century management writer Mary Parker Follett defined management as "the art of getting things done through people."
Liaison	An individual who serves as a bridge between groups, tying groups together and facilitating the communication flow needed to integrate group activities is a liaison.
Synergy	Corporate synergy occurs when corporations interact congruently. A corporate synergy refers to a financial benefit that a corporation expects to realize when it merges with or acquires another corporation.
Evaluation	The consumer's appraisal of the product or brand on important attributes is called evaluation.
Franchise	A contractual right to sell certain products or services, use certain trademarks, or perform activities in a geographical region is called a franchise.
Context	The effect of the background under which a message often takes on more and richer meaning is a context. Context is especially important in cross-cultural interactions because some cultures are said to be high context or low context.
Composition	An out-of-court settlement in which creditors agree to accept a fractional settlement on their original claim is referred to as composition.
Human resources	Human resources refers to the individuals within the firm, and to the portion of the firm's organization that deals with hiring, firing, training, and other personnel issues.
Accounting	A system that collects and processes financial information about an organization and reports that information to decision makers is referred to as accounting.
Command group	Command group refers to a relatively permanent, formal group with functional reporting relationships; usually included in the organization chart.
Task group	Task group refers to a relatively temporary, formal group established to do a specific task.
Task force	A temporary team or committee formed to solve a specific short-term problem involving several departments is the task force.
Committee	A long-lasting, sometimes permanent team in the organization structure created to deal with tasks that recur regularly is the committee.
Ad hoc	Ad hoc is a Latin phrase which means "for this purpose." It generally signifies a solution that has been tailored to a specific purpose and is makeshift and non-general, such as a handcrafted network protocol or a specific-purpose equation, as opposed to general solutions.
Standing	Standing refers to the legal requirement that anyone seeking to challenge a particular action in court must demonstrate that such action substantially affects his legitimate interests before he will be entitled to bring suit.
Autocratic leadership	Leadership style that involves making managerial decisions without consulting others is an autocratic leadership.
Participative management	Participative management or participatory management is the practice of empowering employees to participate in organizational decision making.
Policy	Similar to a script in that a policy can be a less than completely rational decision-making method. Involves the use of a pre-existing set of decision steps for any problem that presents itself.

Internal environment	Variables that are under some degree of control by organizational members is the internal enviroment. Internal environment scans are conducted to identify an organization's internal capabilities, performance levels, strengths, and weaknesses.
Jack Welch	In 1986, GE acquired NBC. During the 90s, Jack Welch helped to modernize GE by emphasizing a shift from manufacturing to services. He also made hundreds of acquisitions and made a push to dominate markets abroad. Welch adopted the Six Sigma quality program in late 1995.
Best of the best	Term used to refer to outstanding world class benchmark firms is referred to as best of the best.
Affiliation	A relationship with other websites in which a company can cross-promote and is credited for sales that accrue through their site is an affiliation.
Teamwork	That which occurs when group members work together in ways that utilize their skills well to accomplish a purpose is called teamwork.
Customer satisfaction	Customer satisfaction is a business term which is used to capture the idea of measuring how satisfied an enterprise's customers are with the organization's efforts in a marketplace.
Profit	Profit refers to the return to the resource entrepreneurial ability; total revenue minus total cost.
Objective setting	Objective setting is the setting of specific goals which are part of the overall business plan for employees to reach. Performance in reaching these goals is outlined, monitored and measured by the organization.
Effective manager	Leader of a team that consistently achieves high performance goals is an effective manager.
Group dynamics	The term group dynamics implies that individual behaviors may differ depending on individuals' current or prospective connections to a sociological group. Group dynamics is the field of study within the social sciences that focuses on the nature of groups. Urges to belong or to identify may make for distinctly different attitudes (recognized or unrecognized), and the influence of a group may rapidly become strong, influencing or overwhelming individual proclivities and actions.
Conflict resolution	Conflict resolution is the process of resolving a dispute or a conflict. Successful conflict resolution occurs by providing each side's needs, and adequately addressing their interests so that they are each satisfied with the outcome. Conflict resolution aims to end conflicts before they start or lead to physical fighting.
Effective groups	Groups that achieve high levels of task performance, member satisfaction, and team viability are effective groups.
Production	The creation of finished goods and services using the factors of production: land, labor, capital, entrepreneurship, and knowledge.
Consideration	Consideration in contract law, a basic requirement for an enforceable agreement under traditional contract principles, defined in this text as legal value, bargained for and given in exchange for an act or promise. In corporation law, cash or property contributed to a corporation in exchange for shares, or a promise to contribute such cash or property.
Productivity	Productivity refers to the total output of goods and services in a given period of time divided by work hours.
Cultural values	The values that employees need to have and act on for the organization to act on the strategic values are called cultural values.
Compliance	A type of influence process where a receiver accepts the position advocated by a source to obtain favorable outcomes or to avoid punishment is the compliance.

Cooperative	A business owned and controlled by the people who use it, producers, consumers, or workers with similar needs who pool their resources for mutual gain is called cooperative.
Turnover	Turnover in a financial context refers to the rate at which a provider of goods cycles through its average inventory. Turnover in a human resources context refers to the characteristic of a given company or industry, relative to rate at which an employer gains and loses staff.
Variance	Variance refers to a measure of how much an economic or statistical variable varies across values or observations. Its calculation is the same as that of the covariance, being the covariance of the variable with itself.
Grant	Grant refers to an intergovernmental transfer of funds . Since the New Deal, state and local governments have become increasingly dependent upon federal grants for an almost infinite variety of programs.
Status congruence	In business, status congruence is the degree to which employers match employee preferences for full-time or part-time status, schedule, shift, and number of hours.
Gain	In finance, gain is a profit or an increase in value of an investment such as a stock or bond. Gain is calculated by fair market value or the proceeds from the sale of the investment minus the sum of the purchase price and all costs associated with it.
Forming	The first stage of team development, where the team is formed and the objectives for the team are set is referred to as forming.
Balance	In banking and accountancy, the outstanding balance is the amount of money owned, (or due), that remains in a deposit account (or a loan account) at a given date, after all past remittances, payments and withdrawal have been accounted for. It can be positive (then, in the balance sheet of a firm, it is an asset) or negative (a liability).
Variable	A variable is something measured by a number; it is used to analyze what happens to other things when the size of that number changes.
Norming	The third stage of team development, where the team becomes a cohesive unit, and interdependence, trust, and cooperation are built is called norming.
Performing stage	The final stage of team developement is the performing stage. Some teams will reach the performing stage. These high-performing teams are able to function as a unit as they find ways to get the job done smoothly and effectively without inappropriate conflict or the need for external supervision.
Empowerment	Giving employees the authority and responsibility to respond quickly to customer requests is called empowerment.
Reorganization	Reorganization occurs, among other instances, when one corporation acquires another in a merger or acquisition, a single corporation divides into two or more entities, or a corporation makes a substantial change in its capital structure.
Termination	The ending of a corporation that occurs only after the winding-up of the corporation's affairs, the liquidation of its assets, and the distribution of the proceeds to the claimants are referred to as a termination.
Adjourning	The stage of team development that involves completing the task and breaking up the team is called adjourning.
Staffing	Staffing refers to a management function that includes hiring, motivating, and retaining the best people available to accomplish the company's objectives.
Team building	A term that describes the process of identifying roles for team members and helping the team members succeed in their roles is called team building.

Quality control	The measurement of products and services against set standards is referred to as quality control.
Controlling	A management function that involves determining whether or not an organization is progressing toward its goals and objectives, and taking corrective action if it is not is called controlling.
Management functions	Management functions were set forth by Henri Fayol; they include planning, organizing, leading, and controling.
Preparation	Preparation refers to usually the first stage in the creative process. It includes education and formal training.
Assignment	A transfer of property or some right or interest is referred to as assignment.
Marketing	Promoting and selling products or services to customers, or prospective customers, is referred to as marketing.
Advertising	Advertising refers to paid, nonpersonal communication through various media by organizations and individuals who are in some way identified in the advertising message.
Preference	The act of a debtor in paying or securing one or more of his creditors in a manner more favorable to them than to other creditors or to the exclusion of such other creditors is a preference. In the absence of statute, a preference is perfectly good, but to be legal it must be bona fide, and not a mere subterfuge of the debtor to secure a future benefit to himself or to prevent the application of his property to his debts.
Trend	Trend refers to the long-term movement of an economic variable, such as its average rate of increase or decrease over enough years to encompass several business cycles.
Contribution	In business organization law, the cash or property contributed to a business by its owners is referred to as contribution.
Argument	The discussion by counsel for the respective parties of their contentions on the law and the facts of the case being tried in order to aid the jury in arriving at a correct and just conclusion is called argument.
Organizational structure	Organizational structure is the way in which the interrelated groups of an organization are constructed. From a managerial point of view the main concerns are ensuring effective communication and coordination.
Aid	Assistance provided by countries and by international institutions such as the World Bank to developing countries in the form of monetary grants, loans at low interest rates, in kind, or a combination of these is called aid. Aid can also refer to assistance of any type rendered to benefit some group or individual.
Margin	A deposit by a buyer in stocks with a seller or a stockbroker, as security to cover fluctuations in the market in reference to stocks that the buyer has purchased but for which he has not paid is a margin. Commodities are also traded on margin.
Market	A market is, as defined in economics, a social arrangement that allows buyers and sellers to discover information and carry out a voluntary exchange of goods or services.
Manufacturing	Production of goods primarily by the application of labor and capital to raw materials and other intermediate inputs, in contrast to agriculture, mining, forestry, fishing, and services a manufacturing.
Compromise	Compromise occurs when the interaction is moderately important to meeting goals and the goals are neither completely compatible nor completely incompatible.

Go to Cram101.com for the Practice Tests for this Chapter.

Leadership	Management merely consists of leadership applied to business situations; or in other words: management forms a sub-set of the broader process of leadership.
Channel	Channel, in communications (sometimes called communications channel), refers to the medium used to convey information from a sender (or transmitter) to a receiver.
Interest	In finance and economics, interest is the price paid by a borrower for the use of a lender's money. In other words, interest is the amount of paid to "rent" money for a period of time.
Jury	A body of lay persons, selected by lot, or by some other fair and impartial means, to ascertain, under the guidance of the judge, the truth in questions of fact arising either in civil litigation or a criminal process is referred to as jury.
Knowledge base	Knowledge base refers to a database that includes decision rules for use of the data, which may be qualitative as well as quantitative.
Effective communication	When the intended meaning equals the perceived meaning it is called effective communication.
Organizational communication	Thee process by which information is exchanged in the organizational setting is organizational communication.
Competitive advantage	A business is said to have a competitive advantage when its unique strengths, often based on cost, quality, time, and innovation, offer consumers a greater percieved value and there by differtiating it from its competitors.
Gain	In finance, gain is a profit or an increase in value of an investment such as a stock or bond. Gain is calculated by fair market value or the proceeds from the sale of the investment minus the sum of the purchase price and all costs associated with it.
Advertisement	Advertisement is the promotion of goods, services, companies and ideas, usually by an identified sponsor. Marketers see advertising as part of an overall promotional strategy.
Vertical communication	Communication between one level of authority and another within an organization is vertical communication.
Chain of command	An unbroken line of authority that links all individuals in the organization and specifies who reports to whom is a chain of command. The concept of chain of command also implies that higher rank alone does not entitle a person to give commands.
Management	Management characterizes the process of leading and directing all or part of an organization, often a business, through the deployment and manipulation of resources. Early twentieth-century management writer Mary Parker Follett defined management as "the art of getting things done through people."
Policy	Similar to a script in that a policy can be a less than completely rational decision-making method. Involves the use of a pre-existing set of decision steps for any problem that presents itself.
Delegation	Delegation is the handing of a task over to another person, usually a subordinate. It is the assignment of authority and responsibility to another person to carry out specific activities.
Upward communication	A communication channel that allows for relatively free movement of messages from those lower in the organization to those at higher levels is an upward communication.
Horizontal communication	The lateral or diagonal exchange of messages among peers or coworkers is referred to as horizontal communication.
Layoff	A layoff is the termination of an employee or (more commonly) a group of employees for business reasons, such as the decision that certain positions are no longer necessary.

Go to **Cram101.com** for the Practice Tests for this Chapter.

Receiver	A person that is appointed as a custodian of other people's property by a court of law or a creditor of the owner, pending a lawsuit or reorganization is called a receiver.
Broker	In commerce, a broker is a party that mediates between a buyer and a seller. A broker who also acts as a seller or as a buyer becomes a principal party to the deal.
Points	Loan origination fees that may be deductible as interest by a buyer of property. A seller of property who pays points reduces the selling price by the amount of the points paid for the buyer.
Face value	The nominal or par value of an instrument as expressed on its face is referred to as the face value.
Trust	An arrangement in which shareholders of independent firms agree to give up their stock in exchange for trust certificates that entitle them to a share of the trust's common profits.
Hearing	A hearing is a proceeding before a court or other decision-making body or officer. A hearing is generally distinguished from a trial in that it is usually shorter and often less formal.
Credibility	The extent to which a source is perceived as having knowledge, skill, or experience relevant to a communication topic and can be trusted to give an unbiased opinion or present objective information on the issue is called credibility.
Nonverbal communication	The many additional ways that communication is accomplished beyond the oral or written word is referred to as nonverbal communication.
Body language	Body language is a broad term for forms of communication using body movements or gestures instead of, or in addition to, sounds, verbal language, or other forms of communication.
Holding	The holding is a court's determination of a matter of law based on the issue presented in the particular case. In other words: under this law, with these facts, this result.
Brief	Brief refers to a statement of a party's case or legal arguments, usually prepared by an attorney. Also used to make legal arguments before appellate courts.
Exchange	The trade of things of value between buyer and seller so that each is better off after the trade is called the exchange.
Productivity	Productivity refers to the total output of goods and services in a given period of time divided by work hours.
Mission statement	Mission statement refers to an outline of the fundamental purposes of an organization.
Evaluation	The consumer's appraisal of the product or brand on important attributes is called evaluation.
Draft	A signed, written order by which one party instructs another party to pay a specified sum to a third party, at sight or at a specific date is a draft.
Media richness	The Media Richness Theory states that the more ambiguous and uncertain a task is, the richer format of media is suitable to it. It is based on contingency theory and information processing theory.
Pleading	In the law, a pleading is one of the papers filed with a court in a civil action, such as a complaint, a demurrer, or an answer.
Assessment	Collecting information and providing feedback to employees about their behavior, communication style, or skills is an assessment.
Excess capacity	Excess capacity refers to plant resources that are underused when imperfectly competitive firms produce less output than that associated with purely competitive firms, who by

definiation, are achieving minimum average total cost.

Empathy	Empathy refers to dimension of service quality-caring individualized attention provided to customers.
Margin	A deposit by a buyer in stocks with a seller or a stockbroker, as security to cover fluctuations in the market in reference to stocks that the buyer has purchased but for which he has not paid is a margin. Commodities are also traded on margin.
Agent	A person who makes economic decisions for another economic actor. A hired manager operates as an agent for a firm's owner.
Federal government	Federal government refers to the government of the United States, as distinct from the state and local governments.
Regulation	Regulation refers to restrictions state and federal laws place on business with regard to the conduct of its activities.
Personnel	A collective term for all of the employees of an organization. Personnel is also commonly used to refer to the personnel management function or the organizational unit responsible for administering personnel programs.
Contract	A contract is a "promise" or an "agreement" that is enforced or recognized by the law. In the civil law, a contract is considered to be part of the general law of obligations.
Brainstorming	Brainstorming refers to a technique designed to overcome our natural tendency to evaluate and criticize ideas and thereby reduce the creative output of those ideas. People are encouraged to produce ideas/options without criticizing, often at a very fast pace to minimize our natural tendency to criticize.
Context	The effect of the background under which a message often takes on more and richer meaning is a context. Context is especially important in cross-cultural interactions because some cultures are said to be high context or low context.

136

Go to **Cram101.com** for the Practice Tests for this Chapter.

Reinforcement theory	A motivation theory based on the relationship between a given behavior and its consequences is referred to as the reinforcement theory.
Corporation	A legal entity chartered by a state or the Federal government that is distinct and separate from the individuals who own it is a corporation. This separation gives the corporation unique powers which other legal entities lack.
Job satisfaction	Job satisfaction describes how content an individual is with his or her job. It is a relatively recent term since in previous centuries the jobs available to a particular person were often predetermined by the occupation of that person's parent.
Turnover	Turnover in a financial context refers to the rate at which a provider of goods cycles through its average inventory. Turnover in a human resources context refers to the characteristic of a given company or industry, relative to rate at which an employer gains and loses staff.
Organizational culture	The mindset of employees, including their shared beliefs, values, and goals is called the organizational culture.
Profit	Profit refers to the return to the resource entrepreneurial ability; total revenue minus total cost.
Henry Ford	Henry Ford was the founder of the Ford Motor Company. His introduction of the Model T automobile revolutionized transportation and American industry.
Ford	Ford is an American company that manufactures and sells automobiles worldwide. Ford introduced methods for large-scale manufacturing of cars, and large-scale management of an industrial workforce, especially elaborately engineered manufacturing sequences typified by the moving assembly lines.
Applicant	In many tribunal and administrative law suits, the person who initiates the claim is called the applicant.
Option	A contract that gives the purchaser the option to buy or sell the underlying financial instrument at a specified price, called the exercise price or strike price, within a specific period of time.
Hierarchy of needs	Hierarchy of needs refers to Maslow's theory that human needs are arranged in an order or hierarchy based on their importance. The need hierarchy includes physiological, safety, social-love and belonging, esteem, and self-actualization needs.
Hierarchy	A system of grouping people in an organization according to rank from the top down in which all subordinate managers must report to one person is called a hierarchy.
Maslow	Maslow was an American psychologist. He is mostly noted today for his proposal of a hierarchy of human needs.
Needs theory	Henry Murray (1893-1988), developed a personality theory during the 1930s up to the 1960s, which he called the Needs Theory. A need in this theory is defined as 'the potentiality or readiness to respond in a certain way under given circumstances'.
Productivity	Productivity refers to the total output of goods and services in a given period of time divided by work hours.
Asset	An item of property, such as land, capital, money, a share in ownership, or a claim on others for future payment, such as a bond or a bank deposit is an asset.
Fringe benefits	The rewards other than wages that employees receive from their employers and that include pensions, medical and dental insurance, paid vacations, and sick leaves are referred to as fringe benefits.

Go to **Cram101.com** for the Practice Tests for this Chapter.

Fringe benefit	Benefits such as sick-leave pay, vacation pay, pension plans, and health plans that represent additional compenzation to employees beyond base wages is a fringe benefit.
Inflation	An increase in the overall price level of an economy, usually as measured by the CPI or by the implicit price deflator is called inflation.
Security	Security refers to a claim on the borrower future income that is sold by the borrower to the lender. A security is a type of transferable interest representing financial value.
ERG theory	Alderfer expanded Maslow's hierarchy of needs by categorizing the hierarchy into his ERG theory. Alderfer categorized the lower order needs (Physiological and Safety) into the Existence category. He fit Maslow's interpersonal love and esteem needs into the relatedness category. The growth category contained the Self Actualization and self esteem needs.
Standard of living	Standard of living refers to the level of consumption that people enjoy, on the average, and is measured by average income per person.
Creep	Creep is a problem in project management where the initial objectives of the project are jeopardized by a gradual increase in overall objectives as the project progresses.
Entrepreneur	The owner/operator. The person who organizes, manages, and assumes the risks of a firm, taking a new idea or a new product and turning it into a successful business is an entrepreneur.
Job Characteristics Model	A conceptual framework for designing motivating jobs that create meaningful work experiences that satisfy employees' growth needs is referred to as the job characteristics model.
Job enrichment	A motivational strategy that emphasizes motivating the worker through the job itself is called job enrichment.
Affiliation	A relationship with other websites in which a company can cross-promote and is credited for sales that accrue through their site is an affiliation.
Gain	In finance, gain is a profit or an increase in value of an investment such as a stock or bond. Gain is calculated by fair market value or the proceeds from the sale of the investment minus the sum of the purchase price and all costs associated with it.
Controlling	A management function that involves determining whether or not an organization is progressing toward its goals and objectives, and taking corrective action if it is not is called controlling.
Authority	Authority in agency law, refers to an agent's ability to affect his principal's legal relations with third parties. Also used to refer to an actor's legal power or ability to do something. In addition, sometimes used to refer to a statute, case, or other legal source that justifies a particular result.
Equity theory	Equity theory, in Business seeks to describe a relationship between employees motivation and their perception of being treated fairly. The theory suggests that employees seek to ascribe values to their inputs and outputs.
Equity	Equity is the name given to the set of legal principles, in countries following the English common law tradition, which supplement strict rules of law where their application would operate harshly, so as to achieve what is sometimes referred to as "natural justice."
Inputs	The inputs used by a firm or an economy are the labor, raw materials, electricity and other resources it uses to produce its outputs.
Supervisor	A Supervisor is an employee of an organization with some of the powers and responsibilities of management, occupying a role between true manager and a regular employee. A Supervisor position is typically the first step towards being promoted into a management role.

Promotion	Promotion refers to all the techniques sellers use to motivate people to buy products or services. An attempt by marketers to inform people about products and to persuade them to participate in an exchange.
Management	Management characterizes the process of leading and directing all or part of an organization, often a business, through the deployment and manipulation of resources. Early twentieth-century management writer Mary Parker Follett defined management as "the art of getting things done through people."
Incentive	An incentive is any factor (financial or non-financial) that provides a motive for a particular course of action, or counts as a reason for preferring one choice to the alternatives.
Contract	A contract is a "promise" or an "agreement" that is enforced or recognized by the law. In the civil law, a contract is considered to be part of the general law of obligations.
Negotiation	Negotiation is the process whereby interested parties resolve disputes, agree upon courses of action, bargain for individual or collective advantage, and/or attempt to craft outcomes which serve their mutual interests.
Warrant	A warrant is a security that entitles the holder to buy or sell a certain additional quantity of an underlying security at an agreed-upon price, at the holder's discretion.
Reference group	A group whose perspectives, values, or behavior is used by an individual as the basis for his or her judgments, opinions, and actions is referred to as reference group.
Complement	A good that is used in conjunction with another good is a complement. For example, cameras and film would complement eachother.
Expectancy theory	A process theory that proposes that motivation depends on individuals' expectations about their ability to perform tasks and receive desired rewards is called expectancy theory.
Valence	Valence refers to the emotional value associated with a stimulus; e.g., a familiar face can have positive valence.
Variable	A variable is something measured by a number; it is used to analyze what happens to other things when the size of that number changes.
Trust	An arrangement in which shareholders of independent firms agree to give up their stock in exchange for trust certificates that entitle them to a share of the trust's common profits.
Operant conditioning	Operant conditioning is the modification of behavior brought about over time by the consequences of said behavior. Operant conditioning is distinguished from Pavlovian conditioning in that operant conditioning deals with voluntary behavior explained by its consequences, while Pavlovian conditioning deals with involuntary behavior triggered by its antecedents.
Standing plan	An ongoing plan used to provide guidance for tasks performed repeatedly within the organization is a standing plan.
Standing	Standing refers to the legal requirement that anyone seeking to challenge a particular action in court must demonstrate that such action substantially affects his legitimate interests before he will be entitled to bring suit.
Privilege	Generally, a legal right to engage in conduct that would otherwise result in legal liability is a privilege. Privileges are commonly classified as absolute or conditional. Occasionally, privilege is also used to denote a legal right to refrain from particular behavior.
Consideration	Consideration in contract law, a basic requirement for an enforceable agreement under traditional contract principles, defined in this text as legal value, bargained for and given in exchange for an act or promise. In corporation law, cash or property contributed to a

Go to **Cram101.com** for the Practice Tests for this Chapter.

corporation in exchange for shares, or a promise to contribute such cash or property.

Continuous schedule	When seasonal factors are unimportant, advertising is run at a continuous schedule throughout the year, we have continuous schedule.
Pygmalion effect	The Pygmalion effect or Rosenthal effect refers to situations in which individuals perform better than others simply because they are expected to do so.
Flextime	A scheduling method that gives employees control over their work schedule is flextime; usually involves some 'core' times when employees must be at work, and a set of 'flextime' that can be adjustable for various employees.
Appreciation	Appreciation refers to a rise in the value of a country's currency on the exchange market, relative either to a particular other currency or to a weighted average of other currencies. The currency is said to appreciate. Opposite of 'depreciation.' Appreciation can also refer to the increase in value of any asset.
Argument	The discussion by counsel for the respective parties of their contentions on the law and the facts of the case being tried in order to aid the jury in arriving at a correct and just conclusion is called argument.
Agent	A person who makes economic decisions for another economic actor. A hired manager operates as an agent for a firm's owner.
Preparation	Preparation refers to usually the first stage in the creative process. It includes education and formal training.

Contingency theory	Any theory that presupposes that there is no theory or method for operating a business that can be applied in all instances is referred to as a contingency theory.
Leadership	Management merely consists of leadership applied to business situations; or in other words: management forms a sub-set of the broader process of leadership.
Management	Management characterizes the process of leading and directing all or part of an organization, often a business, through the deployment and manipulation of resources. Early twentieth-century management writer Mary Parker Follett defined management as "the art of getting things done through people."
Controlling	A management function that involves determining whether or not an organization is progressing toward its goals and objectives, and taking corrective action if it is not is called controlling.
Effective manager	Leader of a team that consistently achieves high performance goals is an effective manager.
Trait theory	An approach to leadership that assumes leaders possess traits that make them fundamentally different from followers. Advocates of trait theory believe that some people have unique leadership characteristics and qualities that enable them to assume responsibilities not everyone can execute. Therefore they are 'born' leaders.
Promotion	Promotion refers to all the techniques sellers use to motivate people to buy products or services. An attempt by marketers to inform people about products and to persuade them to participate in an exchange.
Drucker	Drucker as a business thinker took off in the 1940s, when his initial writings on politics and society won him access to the internal workings of General Motors, which was one of the largest companies in the world at that time. His experiences in Europe had left him fascinated with the problem of authority.
Categorizing	The act of placing strengths and weaknesses into categories in generic internal assessment is called categorizing.
Business ethics	The study of what makes up good and bad conduct as related to business activities and values is business ethics.
Firm	An organization that employs resources to produce a good or service for profit and owns and operates one or more plants is referred to as a firm.
Theory X	Theory X refers to concept described by Douglas McGregor indicating an approach to management that takes a negative and pessimistic view of workers.
Theory Y	Theory Y refers to concept described by Douglas McGregor reflecting an approach to management that takes a positive and optimistic perspective on workers.
Consideration	Consideration in contract law, a basic requirement for an enforceable agreement under traditional contract principles, defined in this text as legal value, bargained for and given in exchange for an act or promise. In corporation law, cash or property contributed to a corporation in exchange for shares, or a promise to contribute such cash or property.
Trust	An arrangement in which shareholders of independent firms agree to give up their stock in exchange for trust certificates that entitle them to a share of the trust's common profits.
Balance	In banking and accountancy, the outstanding balance is the amount of money owned, (or due), that remains in a deposit account (or a loan account) at a given date, after all past remittances, payments and withdrawal have been accounted for. It can be positive (then, in the balance sheet of a firm, it is an asset) or negative (a liability).
Leadership grid	A leadership grid evaluates leadership behavior along two dimensions, concern for production

and concern for people, and suggests that effective leadership styles include high levels of both behaviors.

Production	The creation of finished goods and services using the factors of production: land, labor, capital, entrepreneurship, and knowledge.
Authority	Authority in agency law, refers to an agent's ability to affect his principal's legal relations with third parties. Also used to refer to an actor's legal power or ability to do something. In addition, sometimes used to refer to a statute, case, or other legal source that justifies a particular result.
Trend	Trend refers to the long-term movement of an economic variable, such as its average rate of increase or decrease over enough years to encompass several business cycles.
Charismatic leader	A leader who has the ability to motivate subordinates to transcend their expected performance is a charismatic leader.
Loyalty	Marketers tend to define customer loyalty as making repeat purchases. Some argue that it should be defined attitudinally as a strongly positive feeling about the brand.
Transformati-nal leader	A leader distinguished by a special ability to bring about innovation and change is referred to as transformational leader.
Entrepreneurship	The assembling of resources to produce new or improved products and technologies is referred to as entrepreneurship.
Innovation	Innovation refers to the first commercially successful introduction of a new product, the use of a new method of production, or the creation of a new form of business organization.
Exchange	The trade of things of value between buyer and seller so that each is better off after the trade is called the exchange.
Transactional leader	A leader who clarifies subordinates' role and task requirements, initiates structure, provides rewards, and displays consideration for subordinates is referred to as a transactional leader.
Organizational culture	The mindset of employees, including their shared beliefs, values, and goals is called the organizational culture.
Variable	A variable is something measured by a number; it is used to analyze what happens to other things when the size of that number changes.
Position power	Position power refers to power manager's hold due to their role in the organization. May include a manager's network of contacts, legitimate authority and control over information, rewards, punishments, and the work environment.
Users	Users refer to people in the organization who actually use the product or service purchased by the buying center.
Technology	The body of knowledge and techniques that can be used to combine economic resources to produce goods and services is called technology.
Continuum model	Continuum model refers to a model in which some entities that are normally discrete and exist in finite numbers are modeled instead by a continuous variable. This can sometimes simplify the treatment of large numbers of entities.
Authoritarianism	The belief that power and status differences are appropriate within hierarchical social systems such as organizations is referred to as authoritarianism.
Job satisfaction	Job satisfaction describes how content an individual is with his or her job. It is a relatively recent term since in previous centuries the jobs available to a particular person were often predetermined by the occupation of that person's parent.

External locus of control	The belief by individuals that their future is not within their control but rather is influenced by external forces is referred to as external locus of control.
Directive leadership	Spells out the what and how of subordinates task and expects subordinates to follow orders is called directive leadership.
Internal locus of control	People tend to ascribe their chances of future successes or failures either to internal or external causes. Persons with an internal locus of control see themselves as responsible for the outcomes of their own actions.
Supportive leadership	That which focuses on subordinate needs, well-being, and promotion of a friendly work climate is supportive leadership.
Autocratic leadership	Leadership style that involves making managerial decisions without consulting others is an autocratic leadership.
Participative leadership	Leadership style that consists of managers and employees working together to make decisions is referred to as participative leadership.
Gap	In December of 1995, Gap became the first major North American retailer to accept independent monitoring of the working conditions in a contract factory producing its garments. Gap is the largest specialty retailer in the United States.
Management functions	Management functions were set forth by Henri Fayol; they include planning, organizing, leading, and controling.
Aptitude	An aptitude is an innate inborn ability to do a certain kind of work. Aptitudes may be physical or mental. Many of them have been identified and are testable.
Margin	A deposit by a buyer in stocks with a seller or a stockbroker, as security to cover fluctuations in the market in reference to stocks that the buyer has purchased but for which he has not paid is a margin. Commodities are also traded on margin.
Corporation	A legal entity chartered by a state or the Federal government that is distinct and separate from the individuals who own it is a corporation. This separation gives the corporation unique powers which other legal entities lack.
Productivity	Productivity refers to the total output of goods and services in a given period of time divided by work hours.
Butterfly	In option-trading, a butterfly is a combination trade resulting in the following net position:Long 1 call at (X - a) strike Short 2 calls at X strike Long 1 call at (X + a) strike all with the same expiration date.
Logo	Logo refers to device or other brand name that cannot be spoken.
Contribution	In business organization law, the cash or property contributed to a business by its owners is referred to as contribution.
Inventory turnover ratio	Inventory turnover ratio refers to a ratio that measures the number of times on average the inventory sold during the period; computed by dividing cost of goods sold by the average inventory during the period.
Market share	That fraction of an industry's output accounted for by an individual firm or group of firms is called market share.
Inventory	Tangible property held for sale in the normal course of business or used in producing goods or services for sale is an inventory.
Turnover	Turnover in a financial context refers to the rate at which a provider of goods cycles through its average inventory. Turnover in a human resources context refers to the characteristic of a given company or industry, relative to rate at which an employer gains

Go to **Cram101.com** for the Practice Tests for this Chapter.

and loses staff.

Market	A market is, as defined in economics, a social arrangement that allows buyers and sellers to discover information and carry out a voluntary exchange of goods or services.
Service	Service refers to a "non tangible product" that is not embodied in a physical good and that typically effects some change in another product, person, or institution. Contrasts with good.

Frequency	Frequency refers to the speed of the up and down movements of a fluctuating economic variable; that is, the number of times per unit of time that the variable completes a cycle of up and down movement.
Flexible budget	A budget developed using budgeted revenues and budgeted costs based on the actual output level in the budget period is referred to as flexible budget.
Budget	Budget refers to an account, usually for a year, of the planned expenditures and the expected receipts of an entity. For a government, the receipts are tax revenues.
Operating budget	An operating budget is the annual budget of an activity stated in terms of Budget Classification Code, functional/subfunctional categories and cost accounts. It contains estimates of the total value of resources required for the performance of the operation including reimbursable work or services for others.
Capital budget	A long-term budget that shows planned acquisition and disposal of capital assets, such as land, building, and equipment is a capital budget. Also a separate budget used by state governments for items such as new construction, major renovations, and acquisition of physical property.
Capital	Capital generally refers to financial wealth, especially that used to start or maintain a business. In classical economics, capital is one of four factors of production, the others being land and labor and entrepreneurship.
Financial statement	Financial statement refers to a summary of all the transactions that have occurred over a particular period.
Income statement	Income statement refers to a financial statement that presents the revenues and expenses and resulting net income or net loss of a company for a specific period of time.
Balance sheet	A statement of the assets, liabilities, and net worth of a firm or individual at some given time often at the end of its "fiscal year," is referred to as a balance sheet.
Balance	In banking and accountancy, the outstanding balance is the amount of money owned, (or due), that remains in a deposit account (or a loan account) at a given date, after all past remittances, payments and withdrawal have been accounted for. It can be positive (then, in the balance sheet of a firm, it is an asset) or negative (a liability).
Employee assistance program	Programs offered by companies to help employees deal with job stress and with personal problems that may have developed from the stress or other sources are referred to as an employee assistance program.
Effective manager	Leader of a team that consistently achieves high performance goals is an effective manager.
Controlling	A management function that involves determining whether or not an organization is progressing toward its goals and objectives, and taking corrective action if it is not is called controlling.
Bid	A bid price is a price offered by a buyer when he/she buys a good. In the context of stock trading on a stock exchange, the bid price is the highest price a buyer of a stock is willing to pay for a share of that given stock.
Control system	A control system is a device or set of devices that manage the behavior of other devices. Some devices or systems are not controllable.A control system is an interconnection of components connected or related in such a manner as to command, direct, or regulate itself or another system.
Stakeholder	A stakeholder is an individual or group with a vested interest in or expectation for organizational performance. Usually stakeholders can either have an effect on or are affected

155

by an organization.

Strategic planning	The process of determining the major goals of the organization and the policies and strategies for obtaining and using resources to achieve those goals is called strategic planning.
Operation	A standardized method or technique that is performed repetitively, often on different materials resulting in different finished goods is called an operation.
Standing plan	An ongoing plan used to provide guidance for tasks performed repeatedly within the organization is a standing plan.
Standing	Standing refers to the legal requirement that anyone seeking to challenge a particular action in court must demonstrate that such action substantially affects his legitimate interests before he will be entitled to bring suit.
Preventive maintenance	Maintaining scheduled upkeep and improvement to equipment so equipment can actually improve with age is called the preventive maintenance.
Production	The creation of finished goods and services using the factors of production: land, labor, capital, entrepreneurship, and knowledge.
Inputs	The inputs used by a firm or an economy are the labor, raw materials, electricity and other resources it uses to produce its outputs.
Human resources	Human resources refers to the individuals within the firm, and to the portion of the firm's organization that deals with hiring, firing, training, and other personnel issues.
Stockholder	A stockholder is an individual or company (including a corporation) that legally owns one or more shares of stock in a joined stock company. The shareholders are the owners of a corporation. Companies listed at the stock market strive to enhance shareholder value.
Users	Users refer to people in the organization who actually use the product or service purchased by the buying center.
Buyer	A buyer refers to a role in the buying center with formal authority and responsibility to select the supplier and negotiate the terms of the contract.
Service	Service refers to a "non tangible product" that is not embodied in a physical good and that typically effects some change in another product, person, or institution. Contrasts with good.
Warranty	An obligation of a company to replace defective goods or correct any deficiencies in performance or quality of a product is called a warranty.
Management	Management characterizes the process of leading and directing all or part of an organization, often a business, through the deployment and manipulation of resources. Early twentieth-century management writer Mary Parker Follett defined management as "the art of getting things done through people."
Evaluation	The consumer's appraisal of the product or brand on important attributes is called evaluation.
Customer satisfaction	Customer satisfaction is a business term which is used to capture the idea of measuring how satisfied an enterprise's customers are with the organization's efforts in a marketplace.
Continuous improvement	The constant effort to eliminate waste, reduce response time, simplify the design of both products and processes, and improve quality and customer service is referred to as continuous improvement.
Safety stock	Safety stock is additional inventory planned to buffer against the variability in supply and demand plans, that could otherwise result in inventory shortages.

Inventory	Tangible property held for sale in the normal course of business or used in producing goods or services for sale is an inventory.
Stock	In financial terminology, stock is the capital raized by a corporation, through the issuance and sale of shares.
Manufacturing	Production of goods primarily by the application of labor and capital to raw materials and other intermediate inputs, in contrast to agriculture, mining, forestry, fishing, and services a manufacturing.
Marketing	Promoting and selling products or services to customers, or prospective customers, is referred to as marketing.
Personal selling	Personal selling is interpersonal communication, often face to face, between a sales representative and an individual or group, usually with the objective of making a sale.
Target market	One or more specific groups of potential consumers toward which an organization directs its marketing program are a target market.
Advertising	Advertising refers to paid, nonpersonal communication through various media by organizations and individuals who are in some way identified in the advertising message.
Market	A market is, as defined in economics, a social arrangement that allows buyers and sellers to discover information and carry out a voluntary exchange of goods or services.
Brand	A name, symbol, or design that identifies the goods or services of one seller or group of sellers and distinguishes them from the goods and services of competitors is a brand.
External customers	Dealers, who buy products to sell to others, and ultimate customers, who buy products for their own personal use are referred to as external customers.
Competitor	Other organizations in the same industry or type of business that provide a good or service to the same set of customers is referred to as a competitor.
Training and development	All attempts to improve productivity by increasing an employee's ability to perform is training and development.
Performance appraisal	An evaluation in which the performance level of employees is measured against established standards to make decisions about promotions, compenzation, additional training, or firing is referred to as performance appraisal.
Labor relations	The field of labor relations looks at the relationship between management and workers, particularly groups of workers represented by a labor union.
Labor	People's physical and mental talents and efforts that are used to help produce goods and services are called labor.
Staffing	Staffing refers to a management function that includes hiring, motivating, and retaining the best people available to accomplish the company's objectives.
Financial transaction	A financial transaction involves a change in the status of the finances of two or more businesses or individuals.
Accounting	A system that collects and processes financial information about an organization and reports that information to decision makers is referred to as accounting.
Purchasing	Purchasing refers to the function in a firm that searches for quality material resources, finds the best suppliers, and negotiates the best price for goods and services.
Holding	The holding is a court's determination of a matter of law based on the issue presented in the particular case. In other words: under this law, with these facts, this result.
Asset	An item of property, such as land, capital, money, a share in ownership, or a claim on others

for future payment, such as a bond or a bank deposit is an asset.

Bond	Bond refers to a debt instrument, issued by a borrower and promising a specified stream of payments to the purchaser, usually regular interest payments plus a final repayment of principal.
Fund	Independent accounting entity with a self-balancing set of accounts segregated for the purposes of carrying on specific activities is referred to as a fund.
Revenue	Revenue is a U.S. business term for the amount of money that a company receives from its activities, mostly from sales of products and/or services to customers.
Annual report	An annual report is prepared by corporate management that presents financial information including financial statements, footnotes, and the management discussion and analysis.
Lender	Suppliers and financial institutions that lend money to companies is referred to as a lender.
Product development teams	Combinations of work teams and problem-solving teams that create new designs for products or services that will satisfy customer needs are product development teams.
Product development	In business and engineering, new product development is the complete process of bringing a new product to market. There are two parallel aspects to this process : one involves product engineering ; the other marketing analysis. Marketers see new product development as the first stage in product life cycle management, engineers as part of Product Lifecycle Management.
Firm	An organization that employs resources to produce a good or service for profit and owns and operates one or more plants is referred to as a firm.
Personnel	A collective term for all of the employees of an organization. Personnel is also commonly used to refer to the personnel management function or the organizational unit responsible for administering personnel programs.
Control process	A process involving gathering processed data, analyzing processed data, and using this information to make adjustments to the process is a control process.
Comprehensive	A comprehensive refers to a layout accurate in size, color, scheme, and other necessary details to show how a final ad will look. For presentation only, never for reproduction.
Graduation	Termination of a country's eligibility for GSP tariff preferences on the grounds that it has progressed sufficiently, in terms of per capita income or another measure, that it is no longer in need to special and differential treatment is graduation.
Overhead cost	An expenses of operating a business over and above the direct costs of producing a product is an overhead cost. They can include utilities (eg, electricity, telephone), advertizing and marketing, and any other costs not billed directly to the client or included in the price of the product.
Consideration	Consideration in contract law, a basic requirement for an enforceable agreement under traditional contract principles, defined in this text as legal value, bargained for and given in exchange for an act or promise. In corporation law, cash or property contributed to a corporation in exchange for shares, or a promise to contribute such cash or property.
Critical success factor	Critical Success Factor is a business term for an element which is necessary for an organization or project to achieve its mission.
Success factor	The term success factor refers to the characteristics necessary for high performance; knowledge, skills, abilities, behaviors.
Performance	A report showing the budgeted and actual amounts, and the variances between these amounts, of

report	key financial results for a person or subunit is called a performance report.
Clan control	Control through the development of an internal system of values and norms is clan control.
Organizational culture	The mindset of employees, including their shared beliefs, values, and goals is called the organizational culture.
Policy	Similar to a script in that a policy can be a less than completely rational decision-making method. Involves the use of a pre-existing set of decision steps for any problem that presents itself.
Audit	An examination of the financial reports to ensure that they represent what they claim and conform with generally accepted accounting principles is referred to as audit.
Profit margin	Profit margin is a measure of profitability. It is calculated using a formula and written as a percentage or a number. Profit margin = Net income before tax and interest / Revenue.
Profit	Profit refers to the return to the resource entrepreneurial ability; total revenue minus total cost.
Margin	A deposit by a buyer in stocks with a seller or a stockbroker, as security to cover fluctuations in the market in reference to stocks that the buyer has purchased but for which he has not paid is a margin. Commodities are also traded on margin.
Internal auditing	Internal auditing is a management-oriented discipline that has evolved rapidly since World War II. Once a function primarily concerned with financial and accounting matters, internal auditing now addresses the entire range of operating activities and performs a correspondingly wide variety of assurance and consulting services.
Internal auditor	An accountant employed within a firm who reviews the accounting procedures, records, and reports in both the controller's and treasurer's areas of responsibility is referred to as an internal auditor.
Embezzlement	Embezzlement is the fraudulent appropriation by a person to his own use of property or money entrusted to that person's care but owned by someone else.
Fraud	Tax fraud falls into two categories: civil and criminal. Under civil fraud, the IRS may impose as a penalty of an amount equal to as much as 75 percent of the underpayment.
Economy	The income, expenditures, and resources that affect the cost of running a business and household are called an economy.
Investment	Investment refers to spending for the production and accumulation of capital and additions to inventories. In a financial sense, buying an asset with the expectation of making a return.
Recession	A significant decline in economic activity. In the U.S., recession is approximately defined as two successive quarters of falling GDP, as judged by NBER.
Creep	Creep is a problem in project management where the initial objectives of the project are jeopardized by a gradual increase in overall objectives as the project progresses.
Corporation	A legal entity chartered by a state or the Federal government that is distinct and separate from the individuals who own it is a corporation. This separation gives the corporation unique powers which other legal entities lack.
WorldCom	WorldCom was the United States' second largest long distance phone company (AT&T was the largest). WorldCom grew largely by acquiring other telecommunications companies, most notably MCI Communications. It also owned the Tier 1 ISP UUNET, a major part of the Internet backbone.
Xerox	Xerox was founded in 1906 as "The Haloid Company" manufacturing photographic paper and equipment. The company came to prominence in 1959 with the introduction of the first plain

Go to **Cram101.com** for the Practice Tests for this Chapter.

	paper photocopier using the process of xerography (electrophotography) developed by Chester Carlson, the Xerox 914.
Enron	Enron Corportaion's global reputation was undermined by persistent rumours of bribery and political pressure to secure contracts in Central America, South America, Africa, and the Philippines. Especially controversial was its $3 billion contract with the Maharashtra State Electricity Board in India, where it is alleged that Enron officials used political connections within the Clinton and Bush administrations to exert pressure on the board.
Liability	A liability is a present obligation of the enterprise arizing from past events, the settlement of which is expected to result in an outflow from the enterprise of resources embodying economic benefits.
Management team	A management team is directly responsible for managing the day-to-day operations (and profitability) of a company.
Project manager	Project manager refers to a manager responsible for a temporary work project that involves the participation of other people from various functions and levels of the organization.
Gantt chart	Bar graph showing production managers what projects are being worked on and what stage they are in at any given time is a gantt chart.
Trend	Trend refers to the long-term movement of an economic variable, such as its average rate of increase or decrease over enough years to encompass several business cycles.
Master budget	Master budget refers to expression of management's operating and financial plans for a specified period and comprises a set of budgeted financial statements. Also called pro forma statements.
Statement of cash flow	Reports inflows and outflows of cash during the accounting period in the categories of operating, investing, and financing is a statement of cash flow.
Cash flow	In finance, cash flow refers to the amounts of cash being received and spent by a business during a defined period of time, sometimes tied to a specific project. Most of the time they are being used to determine gaps in the liquid position of a company.
Operating expense	In throughput accounting, the cost accounting aspect of Theory of Constraints (TOC), operating expense is the money spent turning inventory into throughput. In TOC, operating expense is limited to costs that vary strictly with the quantity produced, like raw materials and purchased components.
Expense	In accounting, an expense represents an event in which an asset is used up or a liability is incurred. In terms of the accounting equation, expenses reduce owners' equity.
Acquisition	A company's purchase of the property and obligations of another company is an acquisition.
Capital expenditures	Major investments in long-term assets such as land, buildings, equipment, or research and development are referred to as capital expenditures.
Capital expenditure	A substantial expenditure that is used by a company to acquire or upgrade physical assets such as equipment, property, industrial buildings, including those which improve the quality and life of an asset is referred to as a capital expenditure.
Controller	Controller refers to the financial executive primarily responsible for management accounting and financial accounting. Also called chief accounting officer.
Committee	A long-lasting, sometimes permanent team in the organization structure created to deal with tasks that recur regularly is the committee.
Allocate	Allocate refers to the assignment of income for various tax purposes. A multistate corporation's nonbusiness income usually is distributed to the state where the nonbusiness

assets are located; it is not apportioned with the rest of the entity's income.

Nonprofit organization	An organization whose goals do not include making a personal profit for its owners is a nonprofit organization.
Grant	Grant refers to an intergovernmental transfer of funds . Since the New Deal, state and local governments have become increasingly dependent upon federal grants for an almost infinite variety of programs.
Sales forecast	Sales forecast refers to the maximum total sales of a product that a firm expects to sell during a specified time period under specified environmental conditions and its own marketing efforts.
Fixed cost	The cost that a firm bears if it does not produce at all and that is independent of its output. The presence of a fixed cost tends to imply increasing returns to scale. Contrasts with variable cost.
Variable cost	The portion of a firm or industry's cost that changes with output, in contrast to fixed cost is referred to as variable cost.
Variable	A variable is something measured by a number; it is used to analyze what happens to other things when the size of that number changes.
Cost of sales	Cost of sales refers to the total costs of goods made or purchased and sold.
Total cost	The sum of fixed cost and variable cost is referred to as total cost.
Static budget	Budget based on a single level of output is a static budget.
Incremental budgeting	The process whereby a firm uses current and past budgets as guides and adds or subtracts from these budgets to arrive at the coming period's expenditures is incremental budgeting.
Cost accounting	Cost accounting measures and reports financial and nonfinancial information relating to the cost of acquiring or consuming resources in an organization. It provides information for both management accounting and financial accounting.
Capital asset	In accounting, a capital asset is an asset that is recorded as property that creates more property, e.g. a factory that creates shoes, or a forest that yields a quantity of wood.
Creditor	A person to whom a debt or legal obligation is owed, and who has the right to enforce payment of that debt or obligation is referred to as creditor.
Credit	Credit refers to a recording as positive in the balance of payments, any transaction that gives rise to a payment into the country, such as an export, the sale of an asset, or borrowing from abroad.
Credit market	A credit market is where borrowers come together with lenders to determine conditions of exchange such as interest rates and the duration of a loan.
New economy	New economy, this term was used in the late 1990's to suggest that globalization and/or innovations in information technology had changed the way that the world economy works.
Equity	Equity is the name given to the set of legal principles, in countries following the English common law tradition, which supplement strict rules of law where their application would operate harshly, so as to achieve what is sometimes referred to as "natural justice."
Depreciation	Depreciation is an accounting and finance term for the method of attributing the cost of an asset across the useful life of the asset. Depreciation is a reduction in the value of a currency in floating exchange rate.
Gross profit	Net sales less cost of goods sold is called gross profit.
Net profit	Net profit is an accounting term which is commonly used in business. It is equal to the gross

Go to **Cram101.com** for the Practice Tests for this Chapter.

revenue for a given time period minus associated expenses.

Current asset	A current asset is an asset on the balance sheet which is expected to be sold or otherwise used up in the near future, usually within one year.
Mortgage	Mortgage refers to a note payable issued for property, such as a house, usually repaid in equal installments consisting of part principle and part interest, over a specified period.
Pro forma financial statements	Pro forma financial statements refer to a series of projected financial statements. Of major importance are the pro forma income statement, the pro forma balance sheet, and the cash budget.
Trust	An arrangement in which shareholders of independent firms agree to give up their stock in exchange for trust certificates that entitle them to a share of the trust's common profits.
Productivity	Productivity refers to the total output of goods and services in a given period of time divided by work hours.
Litigation	The process of bringing, maintaining, and defending a lawsuit is litigation.
Regulation	Regulation refers to restrictions state and federal laws place on business with regard to the conduct of its activities.
Labor law	Labor law is the body of laws, administrative rulings, and precedents which addresses the legal rights of, and restrictions on, workers and their organizations.
Theory X	Theory X refers to concept described by Douglas McGregor indicating an approach to management that takes a negative and pessimistic view of workers.
Termination	The ending of a corporation that occurs only after the winding-up of the corporation's affairs, the liquidation of its assets, and the distribution of the proceeds to the claimants are referred to as a termination.
Assignment	A transfer of property or some right or interest is referred to as assignment.
Argument	The discussion by counsel for the respective parties of their contentions on the law and the facts of the case being tried in order to aid the jury in arriving at a correct and just conclusion is called argument.
Competitiveness	Competitiveness usually refers to characteristics that permit a firm to compete effectively with other firms due to low cost or superior technology, perhaps internationally.
Inflation	An increase in the overall price level of an economy, usually as measured by the CPI or by the implicit price deflator is called inflation.
Telecommuting	Telecommuting is a work arrangement in which employees enjoy limited flexibility in working location and hours.
Incentive	An incentive is any factor (financial or non-financial) that provides a motive for a particular course of action, or counts as a reason for preferring one choice to the alternatives.
Industry	A group of firms that produce identical or similar products is an industry. It is also used specifically to refer to an area of economic production focused on manufacturing which involves large amounts of capital investment before any profit can be realized, also called "heavy industry".
Mobil	Mobil is a major oil company which merged with the Exxon Corporation in 1999. Today Mobil continues as a major brand name within the combined company.
Accounts payable	A written record of all vendors to whom the business firm owes money is referred to as accounts payable.

Go to **Cram101.com** for the Practice Tests for this Chapter.

Direct labor	The earnings of employees who work directly on the products being manufactured are direct labor.
Financial ratio	A financial ratio is a ratio of two numbers of reported levels or flows of a company. It may be two financial flows categories divided by each other (profit margin, profit/revenue). It may be a level divided by a financial flow (price/earnings). It may be a flow divided by a level (return on equity or earnings/equity). The numerator or denominator may itself be a ratio (PEG ratio).
Customer value	Customer value refers to the unique combination of benefits received by targeted buyers that includes quality, price, convenience, on-time delivery, and both before-sale and after-sale service.
Aid	Assistance provided by countries and by international institutions such as the World Bank to developing countries in the form of monetary grants, loans at low interest rates, in kind, or a combination of these is called aid. Aid can also refer to assistance of any type rendered to benefit some group or individual.
Gross profit margin	Gross Profit Margin equals Gross Profit divided by Revenue, expressed as a percentage. The percentage represents the amount of each dollar of Revenue that results in Gross Profit.
Turnover	Turnover in a financial context refers to the rate at which a provider of goods cycles through its average inventory. Turnover in a human resources context refers to the characteristic of a given company or industry, relative to rate at which an employer gains and loses staff.
Current liability	Current liability refers to a debt that can reasonably be expected to be paid from existing current assets or through the creation of other current liabilities, within one year or the operating cycle, whichever is longer.
Media market	A media market is a region where the population can receive the same (or similar) television and radio station offerings, and may also include other types of media including newspapers or Internet content.
Contract	A contract is a "promise" or an "agreement" that is enforced or recognized by the law. In the civil law, a contract is considered to be part of the general law of obligations.
Organizational performance	Organizational performance comprises the actual output or results of an organization as measured against its intended outputs (or goals and objectives).
Feedback loop	Feedback loop consists of a response and feedback. It is a system where outputs are fed back into the system as inputs, increasing or decreasing effects.
Expense budget	A budget that outlines the anticipated and actual expenses for each responsibility center is referred to as expense budget.
General manager	A manager who is responsible for several departments that perform different functions is called general manager.
Charisma	A form of interpersonal attraction that inspires support and acceptance from others is charisma. It refers especially to a quality in certain people who easily draw the attention and admiration (or even hatred if the charisma is negative) of others due to a "magnetic" quality of personality and/or appearance.
Supervisor	A Supervisor is an employee of an organization with some of the powers and responsibilities of management, occupying a role between true manager and a regular employee. A Supervisor position is typically the first step towards being promoted into a management role.
Concession	A concession is a business operated under a contract or license associated with a degree of exclusivity in exploiting a business within a certain geographical area. For example, sports

	arenas or public parks may have concession stands; and public services such as water supply may be operated as concessions.
Quick ratio	The Acid-test or quick ratio measures the ability of a company to use its "near cash" or quick assets to immediately extinguish its current liabilities. Quick assets include those current assets that presumably can be quickly converted to cash at close to their book values.

173

Gower College Swansea
Library
Coleg Gŵyr Abertawe
Llyrfgell